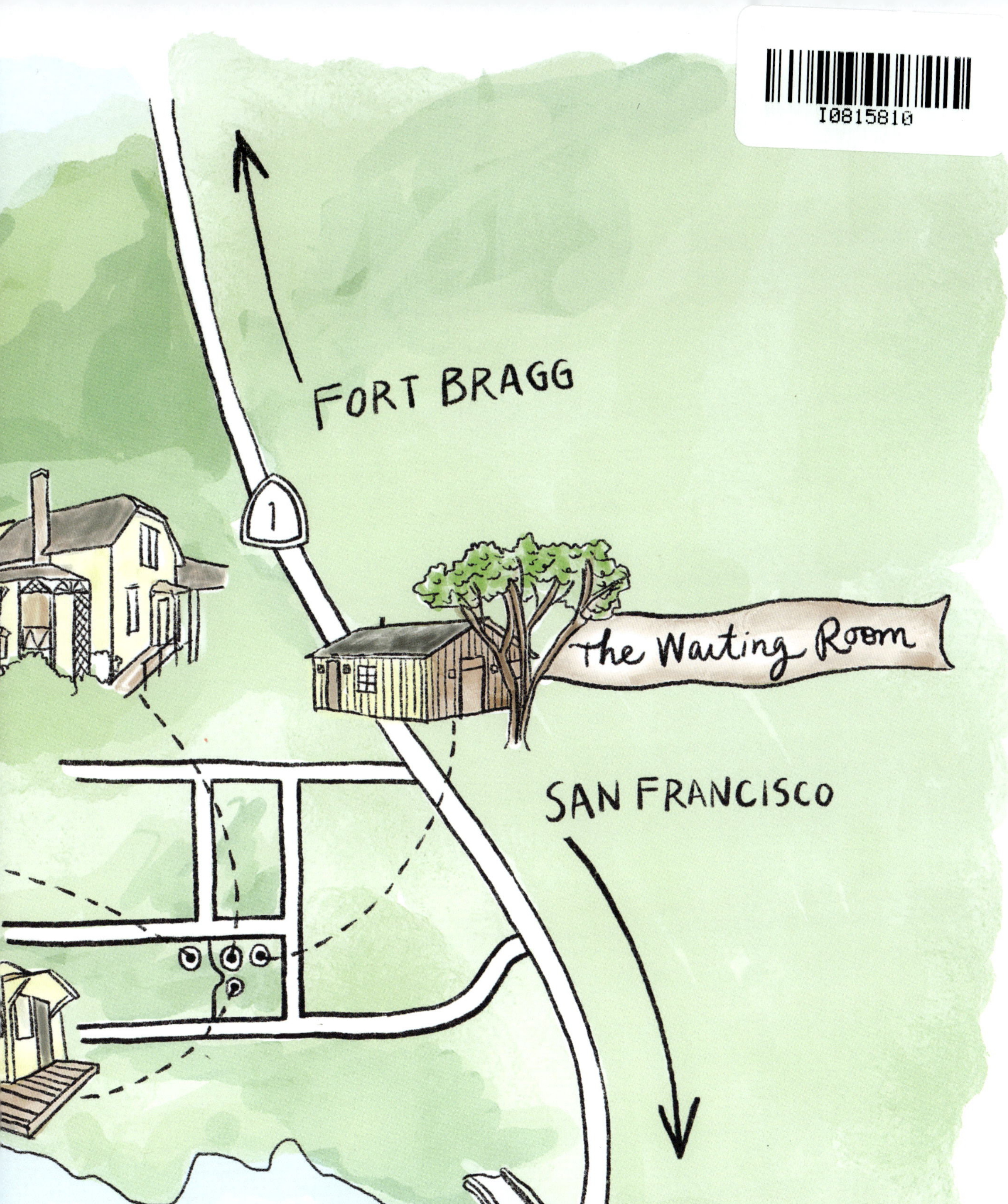
FORT BRAGG
1
The Waiting Room
SAN FRANCISCO
BIG RIVER BEACH

THE NEW
CAFE
BEAUJOLAIS
COOKBOOK

CAFE BEAUJOLAIS

THE NEW CAFE BEAUJOLAIS COOKBOOK

RECIPES FROM THE ICONIC MENDOCINO RESTAURANT

JULIAN LOPEZ

FOREWORD & SELECT RECIPES BY MARGARET S. FOX

Library of Congress Cataloging-in-Publication Data available.
ISBN: 978-1-68555-523-8
Ebook ISBN: 978-1-68555-157-5
LCCN: 2025911430

Manufactured in China.

Art Direction and Design by Rachel Lopez Metzger.
Editing by Jennifer Newens.
Illustrations by Marcella Kriebel.
Photography by Daniela Tallman.
Additional photo credits: Monique Huezo, page 1; Lucille Lawrence: pages 11, 22–25, 71;
Nikolas Zvolensky: pages 12, 50–51, 66–68, 134–135, 163, 188–189, 208, 228, 231–232;
Rachel Lopez Metzger: page 15; John McAllister: pages 134–135; Peter Lopez: page 147;
John Birchard: page 216; Gabi Stryker: pages 226, 252–253; Courtesy of Margaret Fox: page 254.

10 9 8 7 6 5 4 3 2 1

The Collective Book Studio®
Oakland, California
www.thecollectivebook.studio

Contents

Evening Food 145

FOREWORD

As owner of Cafe Beaujolais for more than twenty-three years, it is my pleasure to introduce you to this cookbook, created to continue the Beaujolais legacy by owner Julian Lopez and his wonderful family.

My lifelong fascination with all things culinary is attributed to my own family, where food was a frequent topic of conversation, and much was made of whatever dish had just been prepared by my culinary-obsessed mom.

I made my way to Mendocino from the Bay Area like many people my age, propelled by the desire for something different. After getting my BA at University of California, Santa Cruz, in psychology, I had no immediate interest in pursuing a master's degree. I wanted to be master of my own destiny. I longed for something more "hands on."

It was quite a journey from finishing college to finding my way to the other side of the Redwood curtain to a job at the Mendocino Hotel, where I baked loaves of bread and deep-dish fruit cobblers.

When I heard the Cafe Beaujolais was for sale, three friends and I managed to buy it. Although I knew nobody who owned a restaurant, I had lived in the East Bay when the renowned Chez Panisse opened, as well as Cocolat, a beloved chocolate shop, and Cheese Board, an artisanal pizza shop. I knew what was possible. The can-do mentality of those early years I now see reflected in the inspiration and drive of Julian and his team.

There is a lot to be said for youthful energy. Somehow, improbable things can often be achieved. After six years struggling in a business fueled and financed solely by heart and soul, Ruth Reichl wrote a life-changing review about our breakfasts in *California* magazine. Prior to today's social media, where word spreads faster than syrup on a pancake, there was nothing like the written word to create an overnight success. What a time we had adjusting to being "discovered."

I am so pleased that Julian is continuing the trajectory we subscribed to, with its emphasis on local produce and other ingredients. He has incorporated vignettes of Mendocino's culinary and wine riches in this beautiful book. I love the creativity, curiosity, and energy exemplified by his menus, recipes, and passion for the larger community. We are on the same wavelength, which makes me profoundly happy. Something that has meant so much to me is in good and steady hands.

The Beaujolais experience continues to expand, now including The Waiting Room in a cozy cottage on the corner and Nicholson

House Inn, right next door. You can wake up and meander to The Waiting Room for coffee and pastries, take a walk on the Headlands, have lunch in the garden, visit Russian Gulch State Park or kayak up Big River in the afternoon, and enjoy a nap before an extraordinary dinner at the Cafe. Afterward, circle back to The Waiting Room's cozy evening lounge to chat with fellow visitors and colorful locals.

And there is also The Brickery. Whenever I drive into Mendocino village and see the peaked rooftops of Cafe Beaujolais, I slow down to take in the gardens where diners are picking up handcrafted Brickery pizzas from the wood-fired brick oven, which dates from the days I owned the restaurant. In the morning, local plumbers and tourists head to The Waiting Room for coffee, conversation, or the latest gossip. And dinner is served in the atrium overlooking the garden or in the comfortable dining room of the old house, whose kitchen has served the most delectable cuisine for more than fifty years. I am honored to contribute a few recipes to this book. Recognizing how tastes have changed over the years, I have updated some to reflect this. Fans of old will still recognize their favorites.

To see Julian and his family make an investment and envision the reality that is theirs for Cafe Beaujolais is gratifying. I admire them for interweaving themselves into Mendocino. We choose to create a particular life when we move here and settle in. This sense of place is what makes Mendocino compelling. I can't imagine living anywhere else, especially since that familiar corner at the end of Ukiah Street always welcomes me home.

—Margaret S. Fox

A Note on the Notes

Recipes contributed by Margaret Fox include "MF" under the recipe introduction and identified as "Classic Beaujolais" recipes.

Julian's counter to Margaret's classics are identified as "Modern Beaujolais."

INTRODUCTION

Irrational impetuousness turns into controlled chaos turns into magic.

REMEMBER THAT PLACE I VISITED TWENTY YEARS AGO?

Do you ever have those impulsive moments, where perhaps right in the middle of a boring television show or during a tortured hour of working away on your laptop you sheepishly jump onto Zillow and glance at that house that's perhaps just out of your reach? Or look one last time at that dream property which just went into escrow and you know is now gone forever but you just want to spend a few tortured seconds imagining yourself in that remarkable kitchen or strolling in the dreamy backyard or bathing in the opulent clawfoot tub? It was the spring of 2016 and I was having one of those very moments. However, instead of glancing at that 18th century chalet in Provence or that perfect lake house over a glimmering bay in the San Juan Islands I was looking at boring commercial properties in Mendocino County. Why? I don't know. I had never done that before and it was an unusual impulse for me, but dreaming of Mendocino seemed in hindsight to be an exceptionally fit distraction. Having commuted in Los Angeles traffic for nineteen years at that point, I was seeking big change. Now mind you, I had only been to Mendocino once and that was in 2003. But the feeling I had from that visit had never left me; it gnawed at my psyche every year.

Well, one industrial warehouse here, one abandoned business there, and I was about to leave the website when all of a sudden, a particular listing jumped out at me. The pictures were hazy, almost as if they were meant to dissuade you from taking it too seriously, perhaps purposely shot on a foggy, misty day to attract only the desperate and hardy. One picture after another showed an old house. For the next several days I had the same impulse, perhaps even at the same time every day, where I'd bring up the commercial listing of this Cafe Beaujolais and stare at the slightly off-kilter, almost strange soap box nature of the 19th-century house turned restaurant. The pictures included an overgrown backyard with an old deck as if it were an unkempt European garden ignored since the Victorian age. On one of those dreamy days I timidly called the number on the ad and after initial pleasantries immediately took a liking to the folksy yet sophisticated voice on the line who seemed to feign shock that someone had actually called about the listing. The conversation that began at that moment changed my life and the life of my family forever.

Since then, I've asked myself the perennial question: *What were you thinking?* My wife Melissa has asked the same question a hundred times! This was a town I had visited once on a random weekend trip with friends in 2003. A place my wife and kids had never visited. (But this impetuousness was what I was known for right? For better or for worse these are supposed to be life-changing moments). The recurring memory of driving down Lansing Street in the idyllic village of Mendocino for the first time that day in 2003 had been with me since. I was yearning for a dream I couldn't conjure, and the feeling never went away. Maybe buying that old house with a restaurant in it was the way to fulfill that dream.

In hindsight, however, I've come to realize what really pulled me in, what got it so I couldn't go back, was Cafe Beaujolais itself. She pulled me toward her and there was no going back. . . . So, upon taking the next step and actually visiting Cafe Beaujolais, my infatuation with the concept of taking on this project increased despite the completely obvious hurdles that were immediately apparent. A 140-year-old building, electrical wires hanging all over the basement, a front area off the street looking like a sinkhole. The garden was as overgrown and tired as the pictures had suggested. The kitchen looked like it had seen better days (in the 19th century). But like a surfer who can't say no to the ocean despite no visible waves I couldn't stop thinking about this Cafe Beaujolais. It was like that adolescent crush that completely takes you over. Despite the physical structural flaws and all, the warm, quirky dining room offered something I had never felt. I envisioned fifty years worth of diners looking at me with nodding heads: "Buy it, buy it, it's in your hands now."

BIG CITY NIGHTS TO SMALL TOWN SOLITUDE

None of this would work out—this dream of a country kitchen in the middle of a village in the redwood forest abutting the Pacific Ocean—without the one secret ingredient to pull it off. The first call I made when this whim kept nagging was to my very own son. Who better to persuade to take on an enterprise of this nature than your very own child? It just so happens that my son Julian was an up-and-coming chef in Los Angeles, just starting his culinary career. Who cares if he was only twenty-four years old . . . there was no question of Julian's talent, and his experience up to that point had been particularly unique. Instead of the usual culinary school route he had spent summers in France and Italy gaining experience in several types of kitchens. The only question was why an aspiring chef at the beginning of an auspicious career in the big city would be enticed by the unlikely nature of settling in a town with 1,000 people two hours away from the closest In-N-Out.

WHAT? CAFE BEAUJOLAIS IS FAMOUS?

Up to this point, neither of us knew anything about the wonderful pedigree that Cafe Beaujolais had. We knew it had been open for many years, but it wasn't until later that we realized it was such a cherished part of the community (more on that later). We didn't realize at that time that the Pitzenbarger family had started the restaurant in 1968 and, with three reluctant teenagers, moved from Berkeley to open a restaurant out of the house they lived in (See Eric Pitzenbarger's recent memoir *Beaujolais in My Blood* to learn how this old house similarly drew his family in). We didn't know that the wonderful Margaret Fox purchased the restaurant a decade later and that the beginning of the golden age of "Beaujolais" had begun. Out of the most humble of beginnings, with an eager agenda and an admittedly low budget but a lot of heart, Margaret Fox had turned this cafe into one of the most cherished first-class restaurants on the west coast, if not the nation over the course of twenty years. The advent of "farm to table" had begun, and Margaret was at the forefront of this wonderful culinary approach. The next several years were a whirlwind for the restaurant as it went through its renaissance period, and during this time Margaret had expanded the business to offer Beaujolais merchandise and then wrote the first Cafe Beaujolais cookbook. The cookbook was so wonderfully constructed and made with such compassion and love that it was a big

← 955
MENDOCINO

success and brought the restaurant even more accolades and fame.

But remember, at that time we didn't know any of this, and that's the truth. I can't take credit for a great business decision buying an icon of a restaurant and understanding its history, or seeing the potential of an aged starlet, or whatever decision those who take these endeavors make. This was all about a feeling, a yearning and a desire for something different in my life. This was the furthest away I could get from the freeways of LA and a way to make a go of living in this alluring place called Mendocino. The feeling was long lasting but hard to act on because it seemed based on emotions.

So, this is where my part of the story shifts to what's important: the food, the chef, the team. We did end up buying the place and moving to this wonderful storybook town. And yes, it has been everything we had expected and more. I am not shy or bashful to admit this dream did play out way beyond what I could have ever expected. We really have been all-consumed by Cafe Beaujolais since that fateful decision, and Cafe Beaujolais has been all-consumed by us.

THE SON AND INCREDIBLE TEAM TAKE BEAUJOLAIS THROUGH ITS NEXT CHAPTER

Julian did say yes to my dubious idea after his visit. He talks about his initial thoughts and impressions in another section, but I have been going with the take that "it was his dream" and he "immediately fell in love with Beaujolais." But that would probably be a stretch, and if I was pressed for the actual truth, it would be more like, "What the hell are you thinking, Dad?" The fact is, Julian jumped in head first. He moved to Mendocino, and it has been his effort, passion, and talents that have driven this next chapter of Cafe Beaujolais. That and the efforts of the outstanding staff we inherited, many of whom have been here for longer than our younger team members have been alive. These are tireless, talented people who have felt the same pull to this wonderful institution through all these years.

So, a few weeks had passed since the purchase and announcement that we were the new owners, so we set up our first scheduled meeting to meet the staff. I'll never forget, I walked into a room of thirty people looking at me like I was the executioner who was choosing which one to take to the gallows first. There had been so much uncertainty and fear about the future of the restaurant. But when I got to know the staff one by one and both sides realized the end was not near, I knew that we had a team of devoted people who had been affiliated with this place one way or another for their whole lives, some for a few generations. I realized right away we would just be another caretaker for this wonderful cherished place, and the real owners of the institution were the entire team, the entire community. The Lopez family had not only inherited an old clapboard house but we also had just inherited an institution; we had taken on the responsibility of something way bigger than ourselves. Before I knew any of the history, before I had locals say to me "Oh, you're the new owners of Beaujolais ... don't screw it up," we now knew that our staff was the key to making this whole thing work, and we were in the absolute best hands.

WHAT? THEY ARE DODGERS FANS?

Of course, we encountered furrowed brows from the community after skeptical questions arose about the fact that we were from Los Angeles, and we were trusting the hallowed Cafe Beaujolais to our twenty-four-year-old son. Most certainly people must have thought some young spoiled kid was being handed a gift to play with and that the institution was destined for failure. Indeed, we understood we did have a huge hurdle to overcome on many fronts. But we also knew the kid had what it took to overcome these hurdles and for his talent to shine. Our focus had to be on trying to figure out what it was we had bought and not worry about the smattering of talk around town. Sure, we'd get that sideways glance at the market or a head turn at the post office, but our focus had to be on doing what we could do to make it work. We did just that. Julian proceeded to incorporate his vision into the menu and experiment with different farms and local ranchers. He built relationships with the many vendors who came to the door with blackberries, huckleberries, chanterelle mushrooms, salmon just caught and hanging by giant hooks, bags of porcinis, fresh eggs just hatched an hour earlier at the local farm, and more. We were off to the races.

In the subsequent years we did everything we could to push our vision forward. Julian worked tirelessly and we refined the menu; tried to fit into the community by donating to every money request that came our way (I had never heard of aerial silk dances); figured out where the water pump was and what to do when the water stopped working on a Saturday night with the dining room full; and learned that a condenser breaks down at the worst times, and if you don't have John Ruczak on your speed dial you're not getting it fixed!

INCREDIBLE COMMUNITY

We also found that the community was deeply invested in our success. Invariably every single local person we met had some affiliation with Beaujolais. They either worked at the restaurant at one time or another, had their first espresso at the window, crawled into the cold oven to fix it, ate breakfast there since childhood, or just loved the place and let us know. That devotion helped us immensely, and when we opened up our side window for business the day the Covid panic swept the area, we all had tears in our eyes as the community lined up down the street to buy our smashburgers and Beaujolais Bowls, effectively keeping us afloat. We felt forever bonded and at one with the Mendocino community and will never forget what our customers did for us during that time. We instituted delivery, and between that and the window we were often told we were a beacon of light during the darkness of that period. Importantly, we reopened immediately once the pandemic shutdown occurred and people never forgot.

EXPAND AND EXPERIMENT

Fast forward to today—having endured a hundred-year pandemic, water shortages, pipe breaks, power outages, skunks in the oven, ghost sightings in the residence—we've never stopped learning and trying to refine. One of the first things we realized after moving to Mendocino was that we weren't finding certain things we craved as consumers, so we decided to just make it in house. If customers came, all the better! We took that old English garden that hadn't seen love in a few decades and made the improvements we thought necessary to create a pizza garden, whatever that means. Yes, Cafe Beaujolais had always had a supplementary bakery called The Brickery. We realized quickly that just baking bread wasn't utilizing the amazing oven to its fullest, so we decided to try pizza out of the famous Alan Scott–designed oven (there are only three commercial Scott ovens left in Northern California: Wild Flour in Occidental and Brick & Fire Bistro in Eureka). And off we were with pizza in the garden, also teaming up with our good friends at Wavelength Farms to create "Farm to Pizza." It's probably not good that I have a few pizzas a week, so don't tell Melissa! We also couldn't find the type of coffee that fit our fancy, so we opened a coffee and pastry shop after remodeling the residence and created The Waiting Room. The Waiting Room was designed and built by friends with the sole goal to have a place to hang out with our favorite beer, wine, coffee, and pastries. Again, if you can't find it, build it and hopefully people will show up to help pay for it!

CALIFORNIA CUISINE? WHAT IS THAT EXACTLY?

Ultimately, it always comes down to the food, right? After several years of owning the Beaujolais and debating whether we should keep the famous but oh-so-tired Sturgeon on the menu (a fading starlet and a product of much debate and consternation) or continue to butcher our own hogs (which, due to regulatory constraints, had to be driven 200 miles to the restaurant), we've sought to weave a portfolio of true California Cuisine. Following in the tradition of Margaret Fox's departure from a strict French menu, California Cuisine is what

ATRIUM →
BRICKERY →

it is, with a melting pot of flavors. You will find a whole myriad of ethnic foods at the Beaujolais and can most certainly take a world tour of cuisine in one day. We didn't end up changing the menu too much over the years but have focused on offering a wide array of different types of food, always centered on taste and quality. Julian has said it's not about stars, it's about satisfaction.

ANOTHER COOKBOOK? BUT CAFE BEAUJOLAIS HAS A COOKBOOK AND IT'S FAMOUS!

Time and time again we hear customers say, "we dined here for our anniversary thirty years ago," or "we have come here every year for the last twenty-five years," or even "I was here when the original Pitzenbargers were here in 1972." The twinkle in their eye as they recount these stories brings me back to that first phone call and warms my spirit as I feel some small sense of responsibility for them being able to relive these cherished moments.

When you page through this book you are experiencing a piece of a fifty-five-year legacy. We understand there are not many food establishments that have lasted as long as Cafe Beaujolais has. Certainly restaurants have lives just like we all do: the frailties, hardships, successes, and failures. Cafe Beaujolais has had all of these through the decades but has endured, and we believe the Beaujolais has a special spirit just like Mendocino. As I have repeated, we have felt the force of this institution and we hope this book will allow you to experience this as well, as a bridge to the Beaujolais past through the decades. We are so excited to have Margaret Fox teaming up with us on this endeavor, and her embrace and mentorship of the whole Lopez family have been invaluable and have really helped us in our journey.

This cookbook is our attempt to share this adventure and try to put you, the reader, into this world we found and have continued to nurture and be amazed by. The legacy that Cafe Beaujolais stands for is much more than just a one-time dinner engagement. It's a small slice of life that maybe for the time you are with us either in the Cafe, The Waiting Room, or The Brickery makes your life just a little bit more fulfilling. Perhaps it gives you that food experience that stays with you for the rest of your life like the Beaujolais has for so many people over its existence. Food enhances our lives and takes the human experience to somewhere beyond the daily grind. But food with the right environment, with the right service, in the right location is simply magic. Ultimately, this book is about that magic.

—Peter Lopez

Morning Food

19
OFF
ON
LA MARZOCCO

MORNING FOOD

This chapter explores the two ways to enjoy morning food on the Cafe Beaujolais grounds: a quick, casual breakfast at The Waiting Room and a sit-down Sunday brunch in the Beaujolais dining room. Both meal services evolved to fill a void in town, and in the case of brunch, to revive the legacy of Margaret Fox's celebrated Beaujolais Brunch.

In 2020, we completely renovated the structure adjacent to the main restaurant, which is now The Waiting Room. It was my home for a few years prior, and in Margaret's day, it was the office for her national panforte business. We envisioned opening the intimate space to the community for the first time and remodeled it as a comfortable living room for locals and tourists alike to both enjoy an excellent coffee during the day and sip an aperitif in the evening.

When my Dad and I travel, our first stops are independent coffee shops: places to caffeinate for the day ahead, sink our teeth into regional pastries, and observe locals. Since Mendocino is a tourist destination, it was important to us to create a coffee shop like the ones we enjoy while traveling. We took design inspiration from cozy Alpine lodges, sleek Japanese tea houses, and hip third-wave coffee shops. Music in The Waiting Room is also a critical element of the environment we've aspired to create. Thanks to my Dad, a professional guitarist, guests start their days listening to music on vinyl through hi-fi speakers, cozying up by the wood-fired stove with a cup of Thanksgiving Coffee and a delectable pastry.

Our menu inspiration at The Waiting Room came from Italy's popular espresso bars, combined with the consistency and quality of urban third wave–style coffee shops. We invested in proper equipment, seasonally sourced, high-quality espresso beans, and trained our baristas to dial in the beans and steam milk to perfection. We offer a few sweet and a few savory items, all baked in-house daily.

The morning menu at The Waiting Room is as local and seasonal as it gets. The ingredient essentials for all our baked goods are high-quality, organic, and local whenever possible, including flour and butter from California, and eggs from Mendocino's own Rhizing Ground Farm. The produce available from local farms dictates the flavors of our standard muffins, scones, biscuits, tarts, and galettes: Summer may mean huckleberry muffins; fall may bring butternut squash scones; winter could be orange marmalade–almond croissants; and spring possibly offers rhubarb galettes or cheesy green garlic biscuits. On weekends, we also offer bagels, cooked in our wood-fired oven.

It took some time to conceive and construct The Waiting Room, but when we finally opened its doors at 7 A.M. on December 16th, 2020, we were greeted with the best surprise: Margaret Fox was there as our very first customer!

Shortly after The Waiting Room opened, we were compelled to revive Margaret's legendary brunch. In her era, the Cafe's brunch was a focal point in town—the locals' meeting time and place every weekend. To this day, I still hear new stories about brunch here—it was a special occasion–must from family birthday gatherings to graduation parties. There was the time during a packed brunch service when Margaret called her friend Barry, who lived across the street from the Beaujolais and said, "Barry, your goats have gotten into the restaurant again." Goats in the way or not, Margaret sold out of pastries more often than she didn't. She wrote a book called *Morning Food* in 1989, and most of her recipes were from her beloved brunch service.

While Margaret's brunch was traditional, American-style, and full of delicious pancakes, waffles, omelets, and frittatas, we now play with these classics, adding a multicultural flair. Inspired by Vietnamese, Spanish, French, Mexican, and Tunisian flavors, our twists on the classics keeps customers coming back weekly. While many chefs dislike cooking brunch, I find it a fun opportunity to showcase my cooking style in a more casual format. I can use high-quality ingredients from the previous night's dinner service for brunch specials—such as short rib hash and wagyu or truffles with eggs—and offer them at a more accessible price for guests who want to experience the dining room in a less formal way.

We're humbled by the heaps of annual tourists who still plan a Cafe Beaujolais brunch during their Mendocino visits. And of course, we're thrilled about the continuous support of Margaret's loyal clientele who are exceedingly happy for the return of their brunch.

Mornings at the Beaujolais are truly a community-based experience. Whether you're a local whom our barista cheerily greets by name, or a tourist enjoying a reprieve from a high-volume urban coffee shop, we hope you'll take a deep breath as you inhale the aroma of your custom Beaujolais coffee and savor the start of your day here with us on the Mendocino coast.

Almond Croissants

Almond croissants are one of the simple pleasures in life. I quickly introduced them into my daily morning routine while I worked in France. For the almond croissants at Beaujolais, I added fruit marmalade, whose sweet floral citrus flavor complements the nutty, buttery characteristics of the almonds in these delicious breakfast treats.

MAKES 8 CROISSANTS

SYRUP

2 cups water

1 cup granulated sugar

¼ cup powdered sugar

¼ cup almond meal

2 tablespoons orange blossom water

1 tablespoon vanilla extract

ALMOND CREAM

½ cup almond paste

½ cup powdered sugar

4 teaspoons cornstarch

½ cup unsalted European-style butter, softened

1 farm-fresh egg

1 tablespoon vanilla extract

8 day-old butter croissants

1 cup marmalade (orange works best)

½ cup sliced almonds

Powdered sugar, for sprinkling

To make the syrup, in a saucepan, combine the water, sugars, and almond meal, and set over medium-high heat. Once the mixture comes to a boil, remove from the heat. Stir in the orange blossom water and vanilla extract and set aside to cool. (This syrup can be made in advance. Once cooled, store in an airtight container in either the refrigerator or freezer. It will last up to 2 weeks in the refrigerator and up to 6 months in the freezer.)

To make the almond cream, in a food processor, combine the almond paste, powdered sugar, and cornstarch. Process until well blended. Add the softened butter and blend until smooth, scraping down the sides as needed. Add the egg and vanilla and blend until smooth.

Preheat the oven to 350°F and line a baking sheet with parchment paper.

Create an assembly line with the ingredients: slice the day-old croissants in half lengthwise and set them at your workstation. Next, place a shallow bowl filled with the syrup nearby. Then, set a container with the almond cream and a container of marmalade side by side.

CONTINUED

Almond Croissants *(continued)*

To assemble, dip the cut sides of each croissant into the syrup and hold them there for 5 seconds to allow the croissant to soak up some of the syrup. Place them cut sides up on the work surface. Set aside 2 tablespoons of the almond cream. Divide the remaining almond cream among the bottom pieces of the croissants, spreading evenly. Spread the top pieces of the croissants with the marmalade, dividing evenly. Sandwich the two sides together and place on the prepared baking sheet. Spread a thin layer of the remaining almond cream on top of each croissant sandwich and sprinkle with sliced almonds. Bake until the almonds are golden brown and the croissants begin to crisp up, about 18 minutes. Allow to cool on a rack and sprinkle with powdered sugar. Serve right away.

Beaujolais Fruit Scones

I was never a huge fan of scones until we created these tender delights for the Waiting Room menu. These scones pair perfectly with a warm early-morning beverage. They are a perfect showcase for seasonal fruits. In early spring we take advantage of the rhubarb harvest and then in late spring/early summer we transition to strawberries. Throughout the summer we use wild foraged blackberries and huckleberries. In the winter, we use sliced kumquats. These scones perform really well with frozen fruit, so it's always a good idea to freeze your summer fruit and use it in scones throughout the colder seasons.

MAKES 12 SCONES

- 3 cups all-purpose flour
- 1 cup whole-wheat flour
- ½ cup granulated sugar, plus more for sprinkling
- 1 teaspoon fine sea salt
- 1½ cups cold heavy cream
- ½ cup cold buttermilk, plus more for brushing
- ½ cup cold unsalted butter, cut into cubes
- 1 cup seasonal fruit, such as huckleberries, strawberries, or sliced rhubarb
- Soft salted butter, for serving
- Fruit jam, for serving

Preheat the oven to 375°F. Line a baking sheet with parchment paper and butter the parchment.

On a large, clean cutting board or work surface, combine the all-purpose flour, whole-wheat flour, sugar, and salt and mix well with a whisk. Make a well in the center. Add the butter cubes and, using your hands or 2 rubber bench scrapers, press or cut the butter into the flour mixture until it is the size of peas. Make a well again, and add the cream and buttermilk. Using your hands or the bench scrapers, gently incorporate the ingredients until the dough comes together. Add the fruit and continue to gently bring the dough together. Be careful not to overmix. Form the dough into a disk.

Transfer the dough onto a lightly floured work surface. Using a lightly floured rolling pin, roll out the dough, gently working it forward and backward, side to side, into a round about ½-inch thick.

Using a large knife, cut the scones into triangle shapes and transfer to the prepared baking sheet. Brush the scones with buttermilk and sprinkle with sugar. Bake until the scones are light golden brown, 18 to 22 minutes. Let the scones cool on a wire rack for 10 to 15 minutes. Serve warm or at room temperature with soft butter and your favorite jam. Wrap the cooled scones tightly and store for up to 3 days.

Chai Tea

MAKES 16 SERVINGS

8 cups water
40 whole cloves
22 cardamom pods
20 cinnamon sticks
10 allspice berries
10 whole black peppercorns
8 star anise
Eight ½-inch knobs peeled fresh ginger (about 1 cup)
1 cup sugar
¾ cup loose-leaf black tea
Whole milk or other milk of choice
Ground cinnamon, for garnish

My best friend from middle school was named Saad, and his family was from Pakistan. I spent hours of my formative years at his house doing the many different activities teenage boys do. His house was always perfumed with the incredible smell of spices and curries from his mother's cooking. I would often pop into the kitchen and ask her about the various techniques that she used. One evening, she brought out cups of chai tea. The smell of the exotic spices filled the room as she set the steaming cups on the table. I took one sip and was immediately transported to a place of comfort and ease. The warm liquid was the perfect expression of hospitality. I finished the chai and ventured straight into the kitchen and asked her to teach me the recipe. This is the same recipe she taught me. I hope it brings as much joy to you as it did to me back then.

Put the water into a large saucepan and add the cloves, cardamom, cinnamon sticks, allspice, peppercorns, star anise, ginger, and sugar. Bring the mixture to a boil over high heat, then reduce the heat so the mixture just simmers. Simmer for 10 minutes to bloom the flavors. Turn off the heat and add the black tea. Cover the pot and let the mixture steep for 30 minutes.

Strain the chai concentrate through a fine-mesh strainer into a clean container. Store the concentrate in a mason jar or other container with a tight-fitting lid for up to 2 weeks in the refrigerator.

When ready to serve, heat 1 cup of milk per serving to the desired temperature, add ½ cup chai concentrate to each 12-ounce mug, and pour the hot milk over the chai concentrate. Stir well. Garnish with ground cinnamon and enjoy.

CAFE BEAUJOLAIS
MENDOCINO WILDFLOWER HONEY
CHERRY ALMOND
Granola
Ingredients
Mama (is) Nuts
CAFE BEAUJOLAIS
HOT CHOCOLATE MIX
FROM MENDOCINO
NET WT. 16 OZ. (1 LB.) 454 GRAMS
WILD MENDOCIN
BLACKBERRY JA
Net Wt. 16 oz.
CAFE BEAUJOLAIS
STRAWBERRY JAM
CAFÉ BEAUJOLAIS
PEARSIMMON JAM

www.BeeoQueen.com

CB Products

SUPPLIER SPOTLIGHT

In my early Beaujolais days, when learning everything about the restaurant was like drinking from a firehose, I landed upon an unexpected treasure trove in the restaurant's attic: thousands of blackberry jam labels and empty hot chocolate bags. This discovery was an extraordinary clue in our journey to revive Cafe Beaujolais. Apparently, Margaret Fox's sundries were a big deal, and since whatever worked for her had been a compass toward success for us, we were compelled to carry on the tradition—with our own modern stamp, of course. So just like that, we decided to sell hot chocolate and jam. After all, we couldn't throw away all these iconic (albeit slightly dusty) labels. They were reminders of Beaujolais's heritage, an opportunity to expose our guests to Margaret's history, and transport them to a precious bygone era. We were also excited to offer our extensive tourist clientele delicious Mendocino souvenirs.

We purchased thousands of pounds of luscious, wild Mendocino blackberries from local pickers and fashioned them into mouthwatering jam. To the Beaujolais community's delight, we sold these jars of jam along with hot chocolate bags and a few other goods by the front door of the restaurant. Our sundry program expanded significantly when we opened The Waiting Room, which became the ideal place to display even more products. (Fittingly, Margaret also used this space for her panforte business, another one of her popular sundries.)

Now, every jam and, recently, curd that's served at the restaurant gets jarred for sale. It's fun for guests to take home the pearsimmon (pear-persimmon) jam, which they enjoyed with their foie gras at dinner, or the orange marmalade, which was a component in their chocolate dessert. To go along with these jams, guests can buy our custom rotating Thanksgiving Coffee roast to brew at home. We've also extended the assortment to showcase Beaujolais employees' crafts, including homemade cardamom bitters, hot sauce, and even some printed totes, cards, and hats. Another special sundry, which is a category of its own, is my grandfather's walking sticks. He makes them from local trees—redwood, pine, oak, and cedar—and carves funny faces into them.

Last, but not least, if we had to choose our favorite sundry, it'd be the honey that we harvest from our hives a mere twenty feet from The Waiting Room sundry shelf each summer.

We love that Beaujolais's sundries are a dynamic part of the restaurant that's rooted in Mendocino's seasonality, community, and Margaret's legacy. Next time you're in Mendocino, stop by The Waiting Room to take a bit of our sweet little town home with you.

Dr. Rachel's Pumpkin Muffins

CLASSIC BEAUJOLAIS

These started off as "Rachel's Pumpkin Muffins" in honor of the friend who first introduced them to me when I was at UC Santa Cruz. At the restaurant a few years later, we updated the name to reflect her new professional standing. —MF

MAKES ABOUT 28 MUFFINS

- 2 cups firmly packed light brown sugar
- 1 cup neutral oil, such as safflower, sunflower, avocado, or canola
- 4 large farm-fresh eggs, beaten
- One 15-ounce can pumpkin puree (not pumpkin pie filling)
- 3½ cups all-purpose flour (stir to aerate before spooning into measuring cup)
- 2 teaspoons baking soda
- 2 teaspoons fine sea salt
- 1 teaspoon baking powder
- 1 teaspoon freshly grated nutmeg
- 1 teaspoon each ground ginger, cinnamon, and allspice
- ½ teaspoon ground cloves
- ⅔ cup cold water
- 1 cup coarsely chopped toasted walnuts
- 1 cup raisins or currants

Preheat the oven to 350°F. Line 28 muffin cups with paper liners. (If you need to bake the recipe in batches, just pop the unportioned batter in the refrigerator until needed.)

In a large bowl, mix together the sugar, oil, eggs, and pumpkin. In a separate bowl, sift together the flour, baking soda, salt, baking powder, and spices, and stir to blend. Add the flour mixture alternating with the water (3 additions of flour, 2 of water), whisking just enough to incorporate most of the flour after each addition. Do not overmix. Stir in the walnuts and raisins just until incorporated.

Divide the batter among the lined muffin cups (I like to use an ice cream scoop for ease). Bake until the batter is set and a toothpick comes out clean, about 25 minutes.

Remove from the oven and serve immediately, or let muffins cool in the pan for about 20 minutes, then remove and cool on a rack. Store in a container at room temperature for up to 2 days, or freeze. Defrost and reheat in a microwave (it just takes a few seconds) or in an oven (350°F) for 5 to 8 minutes.

Cream Cheese–Filled Pumpkin Muffins

Make a filling by mixing together 12 ounces natural cream cheese, 1 large beaten egg, ½ cup granulated sugar, and a pinch of fine sea salt until blended. Stir in 7 ounces coarsely chopped crystallized ginger.

Cover the bottom of each lined muffin cup with about 2 tablespoons of the batter, add a generous tablespoon of the filling, then add more batter until the muffin cup is a generous three-fourths full. (An ice cream scoop is especially helpful here to control the mess).

MODERN BEAUJOLAIS

Vegan Streusel Muffins

MAKES 12 MUFFINS

STREUSEL

¼ cup all-purpose flour

¼ cup granulated sugar

2 tablespoons rolled oats

2 tablespoons plus 1 teaspoon coconut oil, at room temperature

¾ teaspoon ground cinnamon

¼ teaspoon fine sea salt

MUFFINS

1½ cups plus 2 tablespoons all-purpose flour

1⅔ teaspoons baking powder

¾ teaspoon ground cinnamon

¾ cup granulated sugar

½ teaspoon fine sea salt

¾ cup oat milk

½ cup olive oil

1 tablespoon fresh lemon juice

1¾ teaspoons vanilla extract

Finely grated zest from ½ lemon

¾ cup blueberries

These muffins were put on the Waiting Room menu in order to provide a vegan option for guests. The muffins are the perfect container for seasonal fruit, but I have found I enjoy the addition of blueberries the most. The streusel component of this recipe does not suffer due to the lack of butter as one might think. These muffins are consistently moist, never dry and are the perfect treat.

Preheat the oven to 350°F. Line a muffin pan with paper liners.

To make the streusel, in a bowl, combine the flour, sugar, rolled oats, coconut oil, cinnamon, and salt. Using your hands, massage the streusel until the mixture resembles wet sand. Set aside.

To make the muffins, in a bowl, sift together the flour, baking powder, and cinnamon. Add the sugar and salt, then whisk until mixed. In a separate bowl, combine the oat milk, olive oil, lemon juice, vanilla extract, and lemon zest. Pour the oat milk mixture into the flour mixture and fold them together with a rubber spatula until the dry ingredients are fully incorporated, taking care not to overmix. Gently fold in the blueberries.

Using an ice cream scoop, portion the batter into the prepared muffin cups until three-fourths full. Divide the streusel mixture among the muffins. Bake until a toothpick inserted into the center of a muffin comes out clean, about 30 minutes.

Remove the muffins from the oven and set on a wire rack to cool for 15 minutes. Remove the muffins from the pan and enjoy warm or at room temperature.

Buttermilk Cinnamon Coffee Cake

CLASSIC BEAUJOLAIS

Oh, this cake! How many thousands of these did we bake over the years? You might think one would become blasé being exposed to the same smell and taste to the point of overwhelm. But no, not with this heavenly cake, sweet and spicy, with the bonus toastiness of walnuts. It was like a "welcome home" every time you entered the kitchen while it was baking. —MF

MAKES ONE 9 BY 13-INCH CAKE

- Unsalted butter or cooking spray for greasing
- 2¼ cups all-purpose flour (stir flour to aerate, then spoon into measuring cup)
- ½ teaspoon fine sea salt
- 2 teaspoons ground cinnamon
- ½ to 1 teaspoon ground ginger
- 1 cup firmly packed light brown sugar
- ¾ cup granulated sugar
- ¾ cup grapeseed oil
- 1 cup chopped walnuts
- 1 teaspoon baking soda
- 1 teaspoon baking powder
- 1 large egg, beaten
- 1 cup buttermilk
- 5 ounces (by weight) blackberries, blueberries, or raspberries, not overly ripe or super juicy

Preheat the oven to 350°F. Grease a 9 by 13-inch cake pan, then line it with parchment paper to form a sling, so the two long sides of the pan are covered by the paper. Grease the parchment lightly.

In a large bowl, mix together the flour, salt, 1 teaspoon of the cinnamon, the ginger, brown sugar, granulated sugar, and oil until thoroughly blended. Transfer ¾ cup of the mixture to a separate bowl, and add to it the nuts and the remaining teaspoon of cinnamon. Mix and set aside to use as the topping.

To the remaining flour mixture, add the baking soda, baking powder, egg, and buttermilk. Mix to combine; small lumps in the batter are okay.

Pour the batter into the prepared pan. Sprinkle evenly with berries, then with the topping mixture (remember the corners). Bake until a toothpick inserted into the center of the cake comes out clean, 40 to 45 minutes. In my experience, ovens have hot spots, so I often turn whatever I'm baking 180 degrees halfway through. However, this cake can fall if moved too soon, so wait until it's baked for 30 minutes before moving, and handle with care.

Remove from the oven and cool at room temperature on a counter for 20 minutes. Once cooled slightly, run a butter knife around the sides of the pan to make sure the cake is not sticking. Cut into square pieces and remove from the pan.

MODERN
BEAUJOLAIS

Almond Olive Oil Coffee Cake

MAKES ONE 9-INCH CAKE

- Olive oil or cooking spray for greasing
- 8 ounces almond paste
- 1⅓ cups granulated sugar, plus 1 tablespoon for dusting
- 1¾ teaspoons fine sea salt
- 5 extra-large farm-fresh eggs, at room temperature
- 1 cup olive oil
- 1 teaspoon vanilla extract
- ¾ cup oat flour
- ¼ cup almond flour
- 1½ teaspoons baking powder
- ¼ teaspoon Maldon salt, for dusting

This cake is one of our bestselling pastries at The Waiting Room at Cafe Beaujolais. It has almost developed a cult following by many patrons who frequent The Waiting Room for their "fix." I hope that once you make this at home you will realize why it has become a cult favorite. It is a simple recipe that delivers a moist, soft, and flavorful cake every single time. It also happens to be gluten free. Enjoy the cake on its own or with a morning cup of coffee or tea.

Preheat the oven to 325°F. Grease a 9-inch springform pan with olive oil or spray and line it with a parchment paper round.

In a stand mixer with a paddle attachment, blend the almond paste, sugar, and salt on medium speed until the mixture takes on a mealy, wet sand consistency, 2 to 3 minutes. Add the eggs one at a time, mixing until each has been fully incorporated before adding the next.

Once the eggs have been fully incorporated, increase the mixer speed to medium-high and beat until the eggs are light and fluffy, about 2 minutes. Reduce the mixer speed to low and slowly drizzle in the olive oil and vanilla extract until incorporated. Turn the mixer off and scrape down the sides of the mixing bowl with a rubber spatula.

In a bowl, whisk together the flours and baking powder until well blended. Using the spatula, fold the flour mixture into the wet batter until it has been completely incorporated and there are no lumps. Transfer the batter to the prepared cake pan and dust with the remaining 1 tablespoon sugar and the Maldon salt. Bake until the cake is an amber brown color and a toothpick inserted into the center of the cake comes out clean, about 1 hour.

Let the cake cool in the pan for 10 minutes, then unmold the cake and invert onto a wire rack. Let cool to room temperature.

Cut the cake into wedges to serve.

Mom's Banana Snack Cake

CLASSIC BEAUJOLAIS

I go through spells of loving bananas, then just as quickly lose interest in them before they're all eaten. By that point, the fruits are very ripe, so I toss them into the freezer where a noteworthy quantity can accumulate. This recipe, a handy way to use 3 or so, produces a fine-textured cake, not the more common (but no less delicious!) classic loaf. My mom included this recipe in her stockpile of what she called "tea cake," which was her description of simple single-layer cakes she whipped up at a moment's notice and served it with a sprinkling of powdered sugar. —MF

MAKES TWO 8-INCH SQUARE OR 9-INCH ROUND CAKES

- Butter for greasing
- 2 cups all-purpose flour (stir to aerate before spooning into measuring cup)
- 1 teaspoon baking soda
- 1 teaspoon baking powder
- 1 teaspoon fine sea salt
- 2 large farm-fresh eggs
- 1½ cups firmly packed light brown sugar
- 1¼ cups mashed ripe bananas
- ½ cup neutral-tasting oil
- ½ cup buttermilk
- 1 teaspoon pure vanilla extract
- 1 cup coarsely chopped, lightly toasted pecans or walnuts
- Powdered sugar, for garnish

Arrange the oven rack to the middle position and preheat the oven to 350°F. Butter two 8-inch square or 9-inch round cake pans. Line the pans with parchment paper and then butter the parchment well.

In a bowl, sift together the flour, baking soda, baking powder, and salt, and stir to combine. In a large mixing bowl (you can use electric beaters for ease), beat the bananas, oil, buttermilk, and vanilla until blended, 2 minutes. Mix in the dry ingredients just until incorporated; do not overmix. Fold in the nuts.

Pour the batter into the prepared pans. Tap the pans on the counter to release any air bubbles, then place in the oven and bake until batter has shrunk from the sides of the pan and a toothpick inserted in the center of the cake comes out clean, about 30 minutes. You can also check by lightly pressing the cake in the center—it should spring back. Remove the cakes from the oven and let sit on a wire rack for 10 to 15 minutes. Run a knife around the outside of the cakes and invert them onto a cutting board or counter and then place onto a serving platter, right side up. Sift powdered sugar over the top for a pretty finish.

Banana Spice Snack Cake

Add 1½ teaspoons of Margaret's Sweet Spice Mixture (page 294) with the salt.

Chocolate Chip–Banana Snack Cakes

Add 12 ounces semi-sweet chocolate chips with the nuts.

CAFE BEAUJOLAIS
961

Vietnamese Fried Rice

MAKES 2 GENEROUS SERVINGS

- 4 garlic cloves, minced
- 1-inch knob peeled fresh ginger, crushed and finely chopped
- 1 shallot, finely minced
- 1 lemongrass stalk, outer layers removed, crushed and very finely minced
- 1 fresh Thai chile, finely chopped
- ½ cup coconut oil or high-smoke-point oil such as grapeseed
- 2 cups cooked short-grain brown rice, spread out onto a baking sheet and cooled to room temperature
- ½ pound (16/20 size) shrimp, peeled, deveined and cut in half lengthwise
- ½ Vietnamese Mother Sauce (page 80)
- ½ pound salmon fillet, cut into ½-inch pieces
- Juice of 1 lime
- ¼ cup chopped fresh cilantro
- ¼ cup ribbon-cut fresh mint leaves
- ¼ cup Thai basil or regular basil
- ¼ cup ribbon-cut shiso (optional)
- 1 or 2 large farm-fresh eggs, fried sunny-side up (see page 292)

Fried Rice has become a fixture on the Cafe Beaujolais brunch menu. Since I have such an affinity for Vietnamese flavors, I developed a California-inspired Vietnamese fried rice dish designed to invigorate diners who may have overindulged the night before. Though the recipe is simple, it does involve a few simple techniques that I recommend perfecting. Like all stir fry–style recipes, this dish requires quick cooking, which is only possible if all of the ingredients are prepped and ready to use within arm's length of the cooking pan.

The keys to success in this recipe are to use short-grain brown rice and to cook it at a ratio of 1 part rice to 1.25 parts liquid. The brown rice holds up well during the cooking process and results in a beautifully textured dish. Contrary to popular belief that the rice for fried rice should be day-old, this rice should be cooked the day you are planning to serve it. Next, cut the vegetables, fish, and shellfish into even-size pieces, which results in a perfectly cooked, finished dish. Nobody wants mushy fried rice! I also like to use an abundance of fresh herbs to brighten the flavors and give a sense of lightness to the finished dish. Finally, top the rice with a perfectly cooked sunny-side-up egg. The runny yolk forms a sauce and creates a contrasting texture to the rest of the dish.

Turn on your kitchen ventilation. Heat a wok or large skillet over high heat until the pan begins to smoke. Once smoking, leave the pan on the heat for another 2 minutes to ensure you have the hottest pan possible.

Meanwhile, in a small bowl, mix together the garlic, ginger, shallot, lemongrass, and chile and set aside.

Add the oil to the hot pan and let sit for 15 seconds. Add the cooled rice and begin to vigorously stir with a flat-edged wooden spoon. Cook, stirring constantly, until the rice begins to brown slightly, about 2 minutes.

Add the garlic mixture to the rice and cook, stirring, for 1 minute longer. The fragrance of the aromatics will begin to rise from the pan as they are heated.

Add the shrimp and stir-fry until the shrimp are starting to turn opaque, about 1 minute. Add the Vietnamese Mother Sauce and the salmon. Stir-fry for an additional minute and remove from the heat.

Add the lime juice, cilantro, mint, basil, and shiso, if using, and stir into the rice, fluffing the grains as you go. Transfer the fried rice mixture to a platter and top with the egg.

Shakshuka

MAKES 4 SERVINGS

CHORIZO

1 pound ground pork

1 tablespoon Spanish smoked paprika

1 tablespoon sweet Spanish paprika

1 teaspoon cayenne pepper

2 cloves garlic, minced

1 teaspoon fine sea salt

TOMATO BASE

1 white onion, finely diced

1 tablespoon fine sea salt

2 cloves garlic, minced

1 tablespoon ras el hanout

1 teaspoon Aleppo pepper

One 28-ounce can crushed San Marzano tomatoes

One 7-ounce jar piquillo peppers, drained and chopped

4 large farm-fresh eggs

Fresh basil, for garnish

While the classic American savory breakfast includes eggs that are cooked in a basic and repetitive form—scrambled, poached, over-easy, or sunny-side up—this recipe is an inventive and playful take on what you might usually expect to see on a breakfast menu. It was created with a traditional North African dish in mind. It has become a mainstay on the Beaujolais brunch menu. Ras el hanout is a spice blend common in North African cuisine. The name is derived from the spice stalls in Morocco where the vendors blend the top shelf spices into their own proprietary blend, though some common components are cumin, cloves, cinnamon, nutmeg, allspice, ginger, chiles, coriander, peppercorns, sweet and hot paprika, fenugreek, and turmeric. This recipe is delicious accompanied by roasted potatoes or a piece of country-style sourdough bread.

Preheat the oven to 350°F.

To make the chorizo, put the pork in a bowl along with the paprikas, cayenne, garlic, and salt. Using clean hands, mix just until the spices are fully incorporated; do not overmix.

Transfer the chorizo mixture to a room-temperature cast-iron skillet and place the skillet over medium heat. Cook to slowly render the fat from the pork, breaking up the meat with a wooden spoon and stirring regularly, until the fat has been released from the pork and the pork begins to take on some color, 7 to 10 minutes. Using a slotted spoon, transfer the chorizo to a plate and set aside.

To make the tomato base, add the onion and salt to the fat in the skillet and cook over medium heat until the onions become translucent, about 5 minutes. Add the garlic, ras el hanout, and Aleppo pepper and sauté until the garlic begins to take on some color, 1 to 2 minutes. Add the tomatoes and chopped piquillo peppers to the skillet and cook over medium heat until the mixture begins to thicken, 5 to 7 minutes. Remove from the heat and fold in the cooked chorizo.

Using the slotted spoon, create four golf ball–sized indents equally spaced in the tomato base. Crack an egg into each indent and place the entire skillet into the oven. Bake until the eggs are cooked to your liking, about 10 minutes, until the yolks are cooked medium. Remove from the oven and let cool slightly before serving.

To serve, sprinkle fresh basil over the top of the shakshuka in the skillet. Use a large serving spoon to divide portions among serving bowls. Enjoy!

Duck Confit & Waffles

MAKES 4 SERVINGS

DUCK CONFIT

1 tablespoon grapeseed oil

4 legs Duck Confit (page 194)

½ cup maple syrup

2 tablespoons butter

WAFFLES

¾ cup unsalted butter

4 cups all-purpose flour

¾ cup granulated sugar

4 teaspoons baking powder

1 teaspoon fine sea salt

6 large farm-fresh eggs, separated

3 cups whole milk

2 teaspoons vanilla extract

As I was developing the brunch menu for Cafe Beaujolais, I wanted to showcase classic American brunch items, but with a twist. This recipe is a riff on chicken and waffles, but I use fall-off-the-bone duck confit in place of fried chicken. The delightfully fatty and crispy duck leg is the perfect counterpoint to the crispy buttery waffle.

Preheat the oven to 400°F. Place a baking sheet on top of the stove to hold the waffles as they emerge from the waffle iron.

To make the duck, warm an ovenproof nonstick sauté pan over medium-high heat. When hot, add the oil and place the duck legs, skin side down, in the pan. Immediately place the pan in the oven and cook until the duck skin is crispy, and the duck meat is warmed through, 10 to 15 minutes. Remove from the oven and place the duck legs on a cooling rack.

To make the waffles, melt the butter in a small saucepan and set aside to cool.

Preheat the waffle iron thoroughly, ideally 15 to 20 minutes before adding the first scoop of batter.

In a bowl, whisk together the flour, sugar, baking powder, and salt. In a separate bowl, whisk together the egg yolks, milk, vanilla, and melted butter. Stir the egg yolk–milk mixture into the flour mixture until incorporated, being sure not to overmix.

In another bowl, whip the egg whites just until they form soft peaks. Fold the egg whites gently into the batter in two additions.

Cook the waffles according to the manufacturer's instructions for your waffle iron. When each waffle is done, place it on the warm baking sheet and cover with foil to keep warm.

Place the sauté pan back over medium heat. Add the maple syrup cook until thickened and reduced, about 2 minutes. Turn the heat off and add the butter.

To assemble, place a cooked waffle on each of four plates and top each with a crispy duck leg. Divide the maple glaze over the duck leg and serve right away.

Rhizing Ground Farm

SUPPLIER SPOTLIGHT

The story behind Rhizing Ground Farm as well as my relationship with its fine founders began in 2017 at neighboring Fortunate Farm in Caspar. Megan Isaacs, a Berkeley graduate with a degree in agriculture, had just stepped into the head farmer role at the farm. She took their business to the next level, increasing their vegetables' quality and yields so they could cater to the local restaurants' sizeable needs. Megan and I built a great relationship in this context, and I was always grateful that she'd grow whatever we wanted for Cafe Beaujolais.

While at Fortunate Farm, where she met her now-husband Cameron Crockett, Megan was intent on starting her own farm business. In 2020, a parcel just east of Fortunate was up for sale. The young couple excitedly purchased the adjacent property and established Rhizing Ground Farm. They've continued growing fantastic summer produce for us—basil, tomatoes, yellow and green squash—but they've shifted their focus to egg production. Megan and Cam saw a gap in the market: no local farms in the area were producing quality chicken eggs at scale. Most local eggs had been sold to home cooks, and if restaurants were lucky, they'd get a few. Lucky for us, Megan and Cam's stellar execution of their vision has meant reliable year-round egg deliveries to Beaujolais.

The ability to buy local, organic, free-range eggs from people I trust was a game-changer for the Beaujolais's operation. Eggs are a critical ingredient in much of our food, notably in our pastries, brunch dishes, pasta, and desserts. Prior to Rhizing Ground's existence, I didn't have any choice but to use whatever generic free-range organic eggs that we could get through a broadline distributor. Undoubtedly, Megan and Cam's unpasteurized chicken eggs, which have never seen a refrigerator, make a huge difference in the quality of our food.

Rhizing Ground prioritizes its hens' quality of life. The hens live stress-free in predator-protected outdoor mobile coops that are moved every 2 to 4 days to a new piece of coastal pasture. The coops feature roll-away nest boxes so the eggs, which Megan and Cam hand-collect and pack daily, stay clean. In addition to whatever they peck as they roam, the hens eat high-quality organic non-GMO chicken feed made from raw whole grains. Megan and Cam take the extra step of fermenting the feed, which offers the hens probiotics and increased nutrient absorption. The better the hens' lives, the more nutritious and delicious their eggs—and we can attest to the fact that Rhizing Ground Farm eggs are, in fact, delicious.

It's no wonder that the plain Rhizing Ground hard-boiled eggs we offer at The Waiting Room sell very well each morning. On weekends, these eggs elevate our omelets and frittatas. Our brioches and custards shine with enhanced complexity and richness thanks to these eggs. Their bright yellow-orange yolks pack bold flavor and wonderful texture, also giving our pasta dough a beautiful hue.

No matter where you live, seeking the best quality local eggs is something you can do to improve your cooking, while also feeling good about supporting local farm businesses.

Beaujolais Benedict

The eggs Benedict at Cafe Beaujolais is not classic in style for a couple of reasons. First, we do not use true hollandaise sauce. Second, we do not use English muffins. Instead, we use a special cheese sauce, a type of Béchamel sauce enriched with cheese, and our house-made sourdough bread. These substitutions create a hearty, California version of the classic brunch dish.

MAKES 4 SERVINGS

CHEESE SAUCE

2 tablespoons minced shallots

2 cups dry white wine

½ cup Chicken Stock (page 294)

3½ cups heavy cream

¾ cup grated Parmesan cheese

¾ cup grated Gruyere cheese

Fine sea salt and freshly ground black pepper

Grapeseed oil

4 slices sourdough bread

8 slices thick-cut ham

2 tablespoons white vinegar

8 large farm-fresh eggs, cracked individually into small cups or bowls

Fine sea salt and freshly ground black pepper

Chopped fresh chives, for garnish

To make the cheese sauce, place the shallots and white wine into a heavy saucepan and bring to a simmer over medium-high heat. Cook until the wine is reduced by half, 7 to 10 minutes. Add the stock and cream. Reduce the heat to medium-low and simmer until the sauce is thick enough to coat the back of a spoon, about 10 minutes. Whisk in the cheeses until fully melted. Taste and adjust seasoning with salt and pepper. Keep warm.

Coat a cast-iron pan with a small amount of oil and place over medium-high heat. Add the bread to the pan and cook until golden brown on each side, turning once, about 45 seconds per side. Remove from the pan and keep warm. Add the ham to the pan and brown it slightly on both sides, about 30 seconds per side. Set aside and keep warm.

Fill a high-rimmed frying pan halfway with water and add the vinegar (the vinegar will help the egg whites coagulate). Set over high heat and bring to a boil. Once boiling, reduce the heat to medium-low so that the water is just simmering. Slowly add the eggs to the water and poach until the whites have cooked and the yolks are still runny, 3 to 4 minutes, or until cooked to your liking.

Using a slotted spoon, transfer the eggs to a paper towel–lined plate. Season the eggs with salt and pepper.

To assemble, place 1 piece of bread on each of four plates. Top each with a piece of sliced ham, two poached eggs, and a generous spoonful of cheese sauce. Garnish each plate with chopped fresh chives and serve right away.

Duck Confit Chilaquiles

MAKES 4 SERVINGS

CHILE SAUCE

- 10 dried guajillo chiles, stems and seeds removed
- 4 dried chiles de árbol, stems and seeds removed
- 4 tomatoes, quartered
- 4 tomatillos, husks removed, rinsed, and quartered
- 4 cloves garlic
- 1 white onion, quartered
- 2 sprigs thyme
- 2 tablespoons fine sea salt
- 1 tablespoon Mexican oregano

- 4 legs Duck Confit (page 194)
- ½ white onion, thinly sliced
- ⅓ cup fresh cilantro leaves
- ½ cup crumbled queso fresco
- 4 large, farm-fresh eggs, fried sunny-side up (see page 292)
- About 4 cups good-quality, thick tortilla chips

The key to delicious chilaquiles is timing. Once the tortilla chips hit the chile sauce you want to eat them as quickly as possible. If you let the chips sit in the sauce for too long you will end up with soggy tortilla chips. In order to achieve the perfect chilaquiles you must have all of your ingredients prepped and easily accessible in an assembly area.

To make the chile sauce, warm a cast-iron skillet over medium heat. When hot, add the guajillos and chiles de árbol. Let them toast in the dry pan, turning them a few times as they cook to ensure they don't blacken, until the chiles are slightly blistered and begin to turn a slight tan color, about 2 minutes. Measure 2 cups of room temperature water into a medium bowl and place the cooked chiles into the water to soften.

Place the tomatoes, tomatillos, and garlic in a saucepan. Fill the saucepan with about 2 cups of water, or just enough to cover the tomatillos and tomatoes. Set the pan over medium-high heat and bring to a simmer. Reduce the heat to low and cook gently until the tomatoes and tomatillos have softened, about 10 minutes. Remove from the heat and let cool slightly.

Add the tomatillos, tomatoes, garlic, onion, thyme, salt, oregano, and chiles with their soaking water to a blender. Blend on high speed until completely smooth, about 30 seconds. Set the chile mixture aside until ready to assemble the chilaquiles. This mixture will last in the refrigerator, tightly covered, for up to 2 weeks and will freeze for up to 6 months.

Remove the skin from the duck confit. Using your hands, pick the duck meat from the bones and shred into bite-size pieces. Set aside. Discard the duck skin and bones.

Set out the sliced onion, cilantro, queso fresco, cooked eggs, and tortilla chips near the stove.

Place the chile sauce and duck confit into a large pot and bring to a simmer over medium-high heat. Once hot, gently fold the tortilla chips into the mixture, taking care not to break them.

Quickly divide the tortilla chip mixture among four plates. Top each serving with an egg and garnish with the sliced onion, cilantro, and queso fresco. Serve right away.

Lunch Food

CAFE BEAUJOLAIS

LUNCH FOOD

Like everything at the Beaujolais, afternoon food here has undergone many iterations over the decades. When we purchased the restaurant, lunch was a formal, white-tablecloth affair five days a week. We wanted to reinvent Beaujolais's lunch service and offer new items that we felt Mendocino's food scene sorely lacked. Notably, there weren't any casual lunch options, which especially appeal to me and my generation, nor good pizza spots in town. Luckily, we inherited a phenomenal brick oven that Chef Chris Kump commissioned from the famous blacksmith, Alan Scott, for his classical French style of bread. The oven sits between the restaurant and garden and is now the heart of our lunch operation.

Given my background in Italian cooking, I was stoked to open a casual pizza window and serve wood-fired, thin-crust Neapolitan-inspired pies. At eight feet long, our oven is significantly larger than the average Neapolitan oven. And while domed ovens reach very high temperatures and yield a quickly cooked pizza with a floppy crust, our arched oven holds a steady temperature that creates an even bake, consistent texture, and perfectly crisp bottom. We fired up the oven with local, neutral-flavored wood, like Madrone and Live Oak, and then perfected our pizza recipe and cooking techniques. Our new pizza window, The Brickery, opened in 2017 as a Friday-to-Sunday lunch spot. The community responded resoundingly to our new casual lunch option, voraciously eating pies in the garden, or grabbing them to go. The overwhelmingly positive response we received quickly led us to add a second daytime offering: smash burgers!

Char-broiled burgers were a big part of my upbringing in Los Angeles. Most people don't realize that SoCal is home to thousands of amazing mom-and-pop burger shops like AstroBurger, Father's Office, Apple Pan, and Pie 'N Burger, just to name a few. I aspired to bring that burger culture awareness to Mendocino—in Beaujolais style, of course. So twice a week, we serve smash burgers—featuring crispy, craggy-edged, juicy, ground beef patties that have been smashed flat over a searingly hot griddle—along with fried chicken sandwiches (another LA cult favorite). We proudly grind our meat for the burgers in-house and serve these delicious bad boys with grilled onions, American cheese, tomatoes, lettuce, pickles, and a house-made special sauce.

We also offer farm-inspired soups and salads for lunch. These aren't your ordinary pizza parlor or burger joint sides. They're all about the fresh produce we source from our friends at Nye Ranch, Wavelength Farm, and Fortunate Farm, and therefore frequently change based on seasonal availability. Even our standard seasonal mixed green salad may look different, topped with beets one week and sunchokes the next.

These experimental daytime menus from The Brickery's takeaway window were a boon when Covid-19 hit and we had to close the dining room. The pandemic forced us to shift our lunch service from the fancy, indoor fine-dining fare to what we really wanted it to be: a casual, relaxing experience in our garden, which filled yet another gap in the community that lacked a public outdoor gathering space.

Our next project was to redesign the Beaujolais garden to resemble its former glory, which rumor has it, was quite the stunner. My Dad's new North Coast friend Lavi, another LA transplant, directed its transformation into more than just a beautiful lunch spot. It became a "secret garden" of sorts: a sacred place tucked away from the busy street for those who want a quiet reprieve among gorgeous blooming plants. The sunny oasis also consists of garden beds full of produce which we use at the restaurant and drought-resistant plants. Folks can hang out at the custom-made outdoor tables, which our good friends, John and Wes, crafted from local, old-growth redwood slabs set on custom cast iron table legs. The bees are always buzzing about, darting between their hives and the cheery giant sunflowers and other pollinator plants. It's special to take in, especially while eating one of our spicy, savory pizzas that are drizzled with our very own honey. In the garden, guests appreciate the close connection between our fertile grounds and our delicious food. They see the abundance of basil and fava beans growing around them that they then consume on our pesto pizza. It's truly a dynamic outdoor dining experience: smoke from the old-school oven wafts through while guests wait for their pies; employees can be seen harvesting produce mid-service; and animated conversations are overheard among the guests, neighbors, and employees enjoying our unique corner of the village.

The Brickery employees and Mendocino locals have created deep relationships over the past several years. Locals were deprived of easy, quick food for so long that they just beam upon arrival, eager to engage, exchange personal stories, and adopt the space as their own backyard. It warms my heart to observe this dynamic almost as much as The Brickery comfort food fills our guests' bellies.

Fall Chiffonade Kale Salad

MAKES 4 SERVINGS

SPICED SQUASH

1 small butternut squash

2 tablespoons grapeseed oil or other neutral-flavored oil

1 tablespoon sugar

½ teaspoon ground cinnamon

¼ teaspoon cayenne pepper

1 teaspoon fine sea salt

Pinch of ground nutmeg

DRESSING

3 tablespoons white wine vinegar

1 tablespoon Dijon mustard

1 farm-fresh organic egg

1 clove garlic

½ teaspoon fine sea salt

½ teaspoon freshly ground black pepper

½ cup grapeseed oil or other neutral-flavored oil

2 bunches kale (preferable lacinato) stems removed, washed, and spun dry

½ cup toasted pepitas

½ cup dried cranberries

½ cup shredded Parmigiano-Reggiano cheese

8 breakfast radishes, thinly sliced

While attending college, I got a job at a local restaurant as a dishwasher. With aspirations of becoming a line cook and then a chef, I figured there was no better place to start than as a dishwasher in a high-volume restaurant. I lasted about eight months washing dishes before moving on to a less physically demanding kitchen position at a restaurant down the street where I could prepare food and let my creative side thrive. Don't get me wrong, I did enjoy my time washing dishes and learned two lessons from my time there. These lessons would prove important to me as I became a chef and a restaurant owner. The first: Always show respect to the dishwasher. They work the hardest job and receive the least amount of recognition from the public, but in reality, they are the foundation of any food establishment. No dishes, no food! The second lesson I took away from this first job was this kale salad recipe. I frequently ate this dish on my break while daydreaming about how one day I would love to highlight this salad on my own menu. This recipe is slightly altered from the original, but it is still the essence of that delectable salad I discovered when I was a dishwasher.

Preheat the oven to 375°F. Place a rimmed baking sheet on the oven rack to preheat.

To make the spiced squash, peel the squash and cut it in half lengthwise. Use a spoon to scoop out and discard the seeds. Carefully cut the squash into ¼-inch cubes—you need 1 cup squash cubes; set the remaining squash aside for another use. In a bowl, toss the 1 cup cubed squash with the oil, sugar, cinnamon, cayenne, salt, and nutmeg until the cubes are evenly coated with the oil and spice mixture. Carefully transfer the squash to the preheated baking sheet. Roast until the squash is tender when tested with a knife, 15 to 20 minutes. Remove from the oven and let cool to room temperature.

To make the dressing, add the vinegar, mustard, egg, garlic, salt, and pepper to a blender. Blend on low speed until fully incorporated. Still on low speed, slowly add the oil: start with a slow drizzle and then gradually increase the flow until you have created a fully emulsified dressing. Set aside.

Several at a time, stack the kale leaves on a cutting board and roll them into the shape of a cigar. Using a sharp knife, cut the roll crosswise into thin ribbons about ⅛ inch thick.

In a salad bowl, combine the kale ribbons, pepitas, cranberries, cheese, and radishes. Using tongs, toss the ingredients while slowly adding the dressing. The salad should look slightly wet but not overly dressed. Taste the salad and add salt and pepper or more dressing if needed.

Divide the salad among plates or bowls and serve right away.

Chopped Salad

MAKES 4 SERVINGS

DRESSING

1 clove garlic

¼ cup fresh lemon juice

¼ cup balsamic vinegar

1 tablespoon fine sea salt

1 tablespoon freshly cracked black pepper

1 cup extra-virgin olive oil

1 pound mixed greens (I like arugula, baby kale, gem lettuce, butter lettuce), cut into thin ribbons

½ pound hearty bitter greens (I like mizuna, radicchio, endive, or frisée), cut into thin ribbons

¾ cup toasted shelled pistachios, crushed with the back of a frying pan or chopped with a knife

1 English cucumber, peeled, seeded, and chopped

1 ripe avocado, peeled, pitted, and diced

1 cup seasonal fruit of your choice: sliced strawberries (spring/summer), sliced Fuyu persimmon (fall), dried cherries (winter)

Fine sea salt and freshly ground black pepper

½ cup shaved Parmigiano-Reggiano cheese

High-quality aged balsamic vinegar, for drizzling

One of the most memorable recipes that I learned early in my career was, of all things, a salad. I was in the middle of a three-month "stage" at Angelini Osteria, a highly regarded Italian restaurant in Los Angeles that serves top-notch northern Italian cuisine. Favorite dishes of customers include complex Lasagne Verde and labor-intensive Agnolotti del Plin, but the dish that has stuck with me the longest is the chopped mixed green salad. The salad-making techniques I learned there helped me form basic guidelines for the salads that I serve at Beaujolais today.

In my mind, there are three ingredients that are key in making a delicious salad. Follow these guidelines at home and you're sure to create a winning salad. First, add nuts or seeds to add texture to your salad. Next, include cheese, preferably a full-flavored cheese such as Parmigiano-Reggiano, feta, Comté, aged cheddar, or another kind to add a contrasting flavor. Finally, include fresh fruit (more common in spring, summer, and fall) or dried fruit (better suited to winter) to add sweetness and tartness to the salad. This recipe has its roots in the salad I learned to make at Angelini's, but I have put my own spin on it. Be sure that the greens are sliced as thinly as possible in order to form ribbons from the leaves. The thinner the slices, the more pleasing textures you will have in your salad.

To make the dressing, add the garlic, lemon juice, vinegar, salt, and pepper to a blender. Blend on low speed until the ingredients are fully incorporated. Still on low speed, slowly add the olive oil: start with a slow drizzle and then gradually increase the flow until you have created a fully emulsified dressing. Set aside.

Put the mixed greens and bitter greens in a salad bowl. Add ½ cup of the pistachios, the cucumber, avocado, and seasonal fruit. Using tongs, toss the ingredients while slowly adding about ½ cup dressing. The salad should look slightly wet but not overly dressed. Taste the salad and add salt and pepper or more dressing if needed.

Divide the salad among serving plates or bowls and sprinkle with the cheese and remaining ¼ cup pistachios. Drizzle servings with the aged balsamic and serve right away.

Green Goddess Little Gem Salad

Green Goddess dressing was first created in San Francisco at the Palace Hotel in 1923. Just like the legend about Caesar salad, this recipe has deep roots in Americana restaurant culture. I am not the biggest fan of creamy, rich dressings that I believe mask the freshness of the greens, but this dressing is the actual star of the salad. The addition of avocado and loads of fresh herbs enhance the vibrance of the little gem lettuce. The anchovies can be omitted if you want the salad to be vegetarian. This makes a lot of dressing, but you can use the rest as a dip for hard-boiled eggs or crudité or as a sauce for grilled chicken.

MAKES 4 SERVINGS

CRISPY SHALLOTS

4 shallots

1 cup peanut, rice bran, or grapeseed oil

GREEN GODDESS DRESSING

1 ripe avocado, pitted and peeled

½ cup mayonnaise

½ cup crème fraîche

1 teaspoon anchovy paste (can be omitted if vegetarian)

½ cup fresh flat-leaf parsley leaves

½ cup fresh basil leaves

2 tablespoons chopped green onion

Juice of ½ lemon

1 tablespoon red wine vinegar

1 clove garlic

1 teaspoon fine sea salt

½ teaspoon freshly ground black pepper

4 heads little gem lettuce, quartered and cleaned

2 purple daikon radishes, quartered and thinly sliced

½ cup shaved Manchego cheese

¼ cup sunflower seeds, toasted

To make the crispy shallots, peel and thinly slice the shallots crosswise. Line a baking sheet with paper towels and set it on a counter next to the stove. Pour the oil into a small saucepan and add the shallots. Place the pan over medium-low heat and sauté, stirring occasionally with a slotted spoon, until the shallots begin to turn a deep golden brown, about 10 minutes. Transfer to paper towels to drain. If not using right away, let the shallots cool and then store them in a container with an airtight lid. They will keep for up to a week at room temperature.

To make the Green Goddess Dressing, in a food processor, combine the avocado, mayonnaise, crème fraîche, anchovy paste, parsley, basil, green onion, lemon juice, vinegar, garlic, salt, and pepper. Process until smooth.

Put the little gem lettuces in a large bowl and add ½ cup of the Green Goddess Dressing. Toss with tongs until all of the lettuce is coated with dressing. Arrange the dressed lettuce on a platter and scatter with the daikon, cheese, and sunflower seeds. Serve right away.

Vietnamese Shrimp Salad

MAKES 4 SERVINGS

VIETNAMESE MOTHER SAUCE

½ cup fresh lime juice

½ cup Vietnamese fish sauce, preferably Red Boat brand

½ cup granulated sugar

1 tablespoon minced garlic

1 tablespoon chopped peeled fresh ginger

1 tablespoon unseasoned rice vinegar

1 teaspoon chopped bird's eye chile

1 pound wild white shrimp, peeled and deveined

1 green papaya

½ cup torn fresh mint leaves

½ cup torn fresh Thai basil leaves

½ cup chopped fresh cilantro

½ cup torn shiso leaves (optional)

1 cup cherry tomatoes, cut in half

Grapeseed, canola, or coconut oil, for cooking

½ cup chopped peanuts

During my travels in Southeast Asia, I became obsessed with the ability of Vietnamese cooks to balance sweet, savory, spicy, and bitter flavors to make a delicious dish. Many of the recipes included what I refer to as the "mother sauce" of Vietnam, a mixture of fresh lime juice, fish sauce, sugar, and aromatics. This sauce captures all of these flavors and allows any protein or vegetable to shine with umami and verve. In this recipe, I use the staple sauce to dress a salad that sings with summer flavors.

To make the Vietnamese Mother Sauce, in a bowl, combine the lime juice, fish sauce, sugar, garlic, ginger, vinegar, and chile and whisk vigorously until the sugar has dissolved. Set aside.

Place the shrimp in a gallon-size locking plastic bag. Measure out 1 cup of the sauce and pour it over the shrimp. Squeeze out the air and seal the bag tightly. Place the bag flat in the refrigerator, making sure that each shrimp is in contact with the dressing. Let the shrimp marinate for a minimum of 1 hour, but preferably 3 to 4 hours.

Peel the tough outer skin from the papaya with a vegetable peeler and discard the skin. Once you have exposed the light green flesh, put the papaya on a flat surface and begin to use the same peeler to create long ribbons of the fruit. Rotate the papaya as you work and do not peel the same section twice in a row. This will allow for even peeling. Transfer the papaya ribbons to a large bowl. Add the mint, basil, cilantro, shiso, if using, and tomatoes, then pour in the remaining sauce. Let the mixture stand while you cook the shrimp.

Preheat a cast-iron skillet over medium-high heat. When hot, add 2 tablespoons oil. In two or three batches, take the shrimp out of the marinade, reserving the marinade, and add the shrimp to the hot oil, being sure not to overcrowd. Cook, turning once, until the prawns are bright pink and are no longer opaque, no more than 2 minutes per side, and transfer to a bowl. Repeat to cook the remaining shrimp. When all of the shrimp have been cooked, add the shrimp marinade into the cast-iron pan and cook until it is reduced in volume by half and has a sticky texture. Pour the sticky mixture over the cooked shrimp in the bowl.

Add the cooked shrimp with the sticky sauce to the bowl with the papaya-herb mixture and toss with the shrimp. Divide the salad among serving plates and garnish with peanuts. Serve right away.

Carrot Ginger Soup

MAKES 8 SERVINGS

- 2 tablespoons virgin coconut oil
- 4 shallots, roughly chopped
- 12 cloves garlic, smashed and finely chopped
- ½ cup finely chopped, peeled fresh ginger
- 1 tablespoon fine sea salt, plus more to taste
- 2 pounds orange carrots, trimmed, peeled, and cut into ¼-inch rounds
- 1 teaspoon ground cayenne pepper
- 1 teaspoon freshly cracked black pepper, plus more to taste
- 2 (13.5 ounce) cans unsweetened coconut milk
- 4 cups low-sodium vegetable broth or water
- 1 cup cold unsalted butter, cut into ½ inch cubes
- Yogurt, sour cream, or extra-virgin olive oil, for serving
- Cilantro leaves, for serving
- Toasted coconut flakes, for serving

The weather in Mendocino tends to be between fifty and sixty-five degrees year round, which is perfect for serving warm and soothing soups. Since I am trained in French and Italian fine dining, I tend to make soups that are blended or pureed over chunkier soups. The flavors in these pureed soups benefit from a last-minute blitz in a blender to allow the flavors to fully emulsify into a lovely, silky texture. In California, carrots tend to be sweetest in the late winter and early spring when they've had a long time to develop in the slow growing season.

Place a stock pot or Dutch oven on the stove over medium heat. Preheat the pot for about 2 minutes then add the coconut oil. Once the coconut oil is fully melted, add the shallots, garlic, ginger, and salt. Sauté until the vegetables begin to soften and become translucent, about 5 minutes. Add the carrots, cayenne, and black pepper and stir to combine. Cook until the carrots begin to soften, another 2 to 3 minutes.

Increase the heat to high, immediately add the coconut milk and broth, and bring to a boil. Once boiling, reduce the heat to low and slowly simmer until the carrots become extremely tender, almost to the point of falling apart, 20 to 30 minutes, depending on the size of the carrots.

Place the hot pot of soup near a blender, preferably a high-speed one. Using a ladle, pour about 2 cups of the carrot mixture into the blender and cover it with the lid. Turn the blender onto the lowest setting. As the soup begins to blend and a whirlpool is created, carefully remove the center piece of the lid, add 4 cubes of butter, and continue to blend. You'll see the soup thicken as it emulsifies. Return the center piece to the blender lid and then blend on its highest setting for 15 seconds. Turn off the blender, taste with a spoon and adjust for seasonings. Pour the pureed soup into a clean pot. Repeat the blending and adding butter steps until you have blended the entirety of the pot. If the soup has cooled slightly, place it back over medium-low heat and heat to the desired temperature (I personally do not like my soup very hot, so I serve it directly after blending).

Divide the soup among serving bowls and garnish with yogurt, sour cream, or extra-virgin olive oil and fresh cilantro leaves and toasted coconut flakes. Serve hot.

Butternut Squash Soup

MAKES 8 TO 10 SERVINGS

- 2 medium-sized butternut squash, cut in half lengthwise and seeds removed
- 1 tablespoon fine sea salt
- 1 tablespoon freshly cracked black pepper
- ¼ cup olive oil
- 4 shallots, cut in quarters lengthwise
- 2 heads of garlic, cloves separated but not peeled
- 8 sprigs thyme

- 8 cups low-sodium vegetable broth or water
- 1 teaspoon ground cayenne pepper
- 1 cup cold unsalted butter, cut into cubes
- Extra-virgin olive oil, for drizzling

I always have a warm feeling in my soul when butternut squash begins to appear in our kitchen at Cafe Beaujolais. It is the time of year when summer turns to fall, the leaves begin to change color, and the days begin to shorten.

Preheat the oven to 375°F.

Place the butternut squash halves onto a baking sheet with the cut sides facing up. Season the squash with the salt, pepper, and olive oil. Divide the shallots, garlic, and thyme into fourths and place them into the seed cavities of the squash halves. Place the baking sheet into the preheated oven and cook for 45 to 60 minutes or until the squash is soft enough to pierce with a knife without much resistance. Once cooked, remove from the oven and place the tray onto a rack to cool.

Place a large pot onto a burner and add the 8 cups of broth and cayenne pepper. Turn the heat up to high and bring to a boil. While the broth is heating, add the cooked shallots. Begin scraping the flesh from the squash with a spoon and add to the broth. Press the cooked garlic cloves out from their skin and add to the broth as well. Once the pot is boiling, turn the heat down to low and simmer for 10 minutes. Turn off the heat and set the pot on a counter near a high-powered blender.

Working in batches, fill the blender halfway with the squash and broth mixture, add a few pieces of butter and blend until smooth. Once smooth, pour into a medium saucepan. Repeat this step until all of the soup is blended.

Serve with a drizzle of olive oil and enjoy.

Wavelength Farm

SUPPLIER SPOTLIGHT

One of the things that makes my relationship with Mendocino so special is that Cafe Beaujolais has grown in tandem with other small local businesses. Wavelength Farm is one of those businesses and one of my favorite producer partners. My now good friend, Kelan Daniel, established Wavelength soon after we purchased Beaujolais. Our dads also became fast friends upon moving here around the same time.

Wavelength is a 100-acre diversified farm and ranch in Manchester, about thirty miles from Mendocino. They steward their gardens and pastures through innovative and regenerative farming practices and focus on ecology education. Notably, they only sow rare organic heirloom varieties of produce, coaxing remarkable flavor from everything they grow. They have three different microclimates on their farm that enable them to cultivate an amazing diversity of produce.

Their unbelievably tasty Albion strawberries are among my favorite Wavelength discoveries. These meaty, earthy, yet sweet flavor bombs grow in cold climates, where the slow development enhances their complex flavors. Wavelength Farm also specializes in greens. We rely on their interesting varieties of hearty braising greens, such as heirloom choys I hadn't heard of until Kelan introduced them to me. Their leafy salad mix is an elaborate bouquet of greens you can't really find elsewhere. In the summer, their tomatoes, peppers, eggplants, and legendary shishito peppers make our dishes sing. We primarily use Wavelength's produce for our easily adaptable pizza menu since they prioritize variety and quality over quantity. We're very fortunate to serve unique pies that are hyper-focused on delicious organic heirloom vegetables. The best Wavelength showcase is our ever-changing vegan pizza featuring a medley of their seasonal vegetables that we roast to perfection in our wood-fired oven.

When The Brickery's garden filled with guests enjoying Wavelength produce-topped pizzas, we wanted to enhance the outdoor dining space. So, in 2018, we approached Kelan about creating a farmstand on the grounds. The following year Kelan's father, Lavi, a landscape architect, redesigned the Beaujolais garden to become the oasis it is today. Kelan happily built a sweet structure that holds the Wavelength produce, providing them with a consistent revenue center at a community hub in town. In true small-town fashion, buying Wavelength's incredible produce is on the honor system. While the farmstand no longer stands, we have fond memories of locals enjoying its bounty as they waited for their pizza order in the garden.

Mexican-Style Pork & Hominy Soup (Not Posole!)

This recipe explores how to properly use dried whole Mexican chiles. A list of the various dried chiles could take up the entirety of this book, but for ease of use and accessibility, I focus on the few chiles that are readily available in markets in the U.S. Dried chiles, similarly to dried spices, benefit from a toasting or roasting before using. This technique concentrates the natural flavors and adds smoky, charred nuances. The chipotle meco chiles I use in this recipe in particular benefit from this toasting and charring, and in my mind bring loads more flavor than your typical chipotle peppers in adobo that you find in most recipes. Look for them in Latin markets or from an online source. This is a soup that gets better with time. In my experience, the third day after simmering showcases the flavors best. This recipe is not technically a posole due to the addition of ingredients such as carrots, potatoes, and tomatoes. I like to add these ingredients for more flavor and heartiness than your typical posole.

MAKES 8 SERVINGS

CHILE BASE

- 5 dried ancho chiles
- 2 dried chipotle meco chiles
- 4 dried chiles de arbol
- 5 dried morita chiles
- 2 tablespoons high-smoke-point oil, such as grapeseed or peanut
- 4 garlic cloves, roughly chopped
- 1 white onion, diced
- 4 whole cloves
- 2 tablespoons Mexican oregano
- 1 tablespoon ground cinnamon
- 1 tablespoon whole cumin seeds
- 8 medium-size fresh tomatillos, husks removed and rinsed
- 1 (28-ounce) can whole peeled San Marzano tomatoes
- 12 cups water or low-sodium beef stock
- ½ cup freshly squeezed orange juice
- ½ cup high-quality honey, preferably local
- 2 tablespoons fine sea salt

CONTINUED

To make the chile base, remove the stems from the ancho chiles, then shake out the seeds into a bowl. Repeat with the chipotle, chiles de árbol, and chiles morita, collecting the seeds in the same bowl.

Turn on your kitchen ventilation and open a window, if possible; toasting the chiles, especially the seeds, will release strong aromas. Warm a heavy cast-iron skillet over high heat until very hot. Working in batches, add the chiles to the pan, being careful not to crowd the skillet. Cook the chiles, turning with tongs as needed, until just brown and toasted, and each chile begins to smoke. If the skillet is hot enough, this should take less than 30 seconds per side. Transfer the chiles to a plate. Repeat with the remaining chiles.

CONTINUED

Mexican-Style Pork & Hominy Soup *(continued)*

- 5 pounds boneless pork shoulder, cut into 1-inch chunks
- 1 (12-ounce) can or bottle light Mexican lager, such as Pacifico or Modelo Especial
- 2 large carrots, peeled and cut into 1-inch chunks
- 1 yellow onion, peeled and cut into large dice
- 2 cups fingerling potatoes, cleaned and halved lengthwise
- 1 (29-ounce) can hominy, drained and rinsed
- Shredded green cabbage, sliced radishes, and lime wedges, for serving

In a large pot over medium heat, add the chile seeds. Cook, stirring, until the seeds are toasted and very aromatic, about 1 minute. Add the oil, garlic, onion, cloves, oregano, cinnamon, and cumin seeds and cook until the onion is translucent, 3 to 5 minutes. Add the tomatillos, tomatoes, water or stock, orange juice, honey, and salt. Increase the heat to high and bring the mixture to a boil. Reduce the heat to low and simmer until the tomatillos turn a pale green color, about 5 minutes.

Using an immersion blender, carefully blend all of the ingredients in the pot until smooth. (Alternatively, for a smoother texture, use a high-speed blender to puree the mixture in batches.) Let the mixture cool. If not using right away, you can refrigerate the chile base for up to 1 week or freeze it for up to 3 months.

To make the soup, warm a large Dutch oven or heavy-bottomed pot over medium-high heat and line a rimmed baking sheet with paper towels. Add one-third of the pork to the pot and cook until well browned on all sides, 4 to 5 minutes per side. Transfer the browned pork to the towel-lined baking sheet. Repeat to brown the remaining pork in two batches.

Pour off the rendered fat in the pot. Add the beer to the pot, scraping the charred tasty bits from the bottom. Add the carrots, onions, potatoes, browned pork, and the chile base. Place over medium heat and bring the mixture just to a boil, then reduce the heat to low and simmer until the pork is tender and the vegetables are cooked through, 1 to 2 hours.

Add the drained and rinsed hominy to the soup and simmer until the hominy is heated through and begins to soak up some of the soup's flavor, about 15 minutes.

Divide the soup among large bowls and top with sliced cabbage and radish slices. Set out the lime wedges for squeezing over the soup.

CLASSIC BEAUJOLAIS

Original Cafe Beaujolais Tomato Bisque

MAKES 6 TO 8 SERVINGS

- ½ cup chopped yellow onions
- ½ cup (8 tablespoons) unsalted butter
- 1 teaspoon dried dill seed
- 1½ teaspoons dried dill
- 1½ teaspoons Beaujolais Blend Herbs (page 292)
- 5 cups whole canned tomatoes, crushed
- 4 cups Chicken Stock (page 294)
- 2 tablespoons all-purpose flour
- 2 teaspoons kosher salt
- ½ teaspoon ground white pepper
- ¼ cup chopped fresh parsley
- 4 teaspoons honey
- 1¼ cups heavy cream
- ⅔ cup half-and-half
- Sour cream, for garnish
- 6 to 8 small fresh basil leaves, for garnish

Perfect for our coastal climate, which is often overcast and chilly, this comforting soup is sublimely rich, kind of like wrapping yourself in a cashmere sweater. I was pretty stunned when I looked at my recipes from years ago and saw how rich a lot of them were. With abandon, I added butter, sour cream, whipping cream, and crème fraîche generously to many recipes. These days, my palate and preference run more to flavor than fat, at least fat for fat's sake. But this is still a lovely recipe, and who doesn't like to indulge every once in a while? —MF

In a large pot over medium-high heat, sauté the onions in 6 tablespoons of the butter along with the dill seed, dried dill, and herb blend until the onions are translucent, about 5 minutes. Add the tomatoes and chicken stock and leave on the stove to heat.

In a small pan, make a roux by blending the remaining 2 tablespoons of the butter with the flour, whisking constantly over medium heat for 3 minutes, without browning. Add the roux to the stock mixture and whisk to blend. Add the salt and pepper. Bring to a boil, stirring occasionally. Reduce the heat and simmer for 15 minutes. Add the chopped parsley, honey, cream, and half-and-half. Remove the pan from the heat.

Insert an immersion blender into the soup and puree until smooth, taking care to keep the blender submerged in the liquid at all times to avoid splatters. (Alternatively, working in batches, if necessary, carefully transfer the hot soup to a blender and puree until smooth.) Strain the soup through a fine to medium sieve into a clean pot. When ready to serve, reheat, divide among soup bowls, and garnish each serving with a small dollop of sour cream and a fresh basil leaf.

Roasted Tomato Bisque

MODERN BEAUJOLAIS

One would imagine the cool, foggy Mendocino coast would not have a warm enough growing season to allow tomatoes to ripen. To my surprise, the majority of our local farms have an abundant tomato harvest. Starting in early August through the month of October, we are inundated with large quantities of tomatoes from our local farms. We at Beaujolais use this time of the year to highlight tomatoes in many of our dishes. This roasted tomato bisque is a mainstay on our menu during the late summer and early fall months. It is a perfect way to use up a large tomato crop and warms the soul on our cool, foggy summer days. Of course, the best thing to serve with any kind of tomato soup is a grilled cheese sandwich, ideally between slices of California sourdough bread.

MAKES 4 SERVINGS

3 pounds fresh tomatoes, cut in half

¾ cup extra-virgin olive oil, plus more for drizzling

1 tablespoon dried oregano

1 tablespoon fine sea salt, plus more for garnish

1 teaspoon red pepper flakes

1 head garlic, skin on and halved horizontally

2 shallots, peeled and halved

4 cups homemade Chicken Stock (page 294) or low-sodium vegetable broth

6 basil leaves, plus shredded basil leaves for garnish

Preheat the oven to 325°F.

Arrange the tomato halves in a single layer on one or more rimmed baking sheets. Drizzle the tomatoes with ½ cup of the olive oil and season with oregano, salt, and red pepper flakes. Nestle the garlic and shallots in between the tomatoes on the baking sheet. Place the baking sheet(s) in the oven and roast until the tomatoes begin to caramelize and the garlic becomes soft and spreadable like butter, 60 to 90 minutes. Remove from the oven and set aside.

Pour the chicken or vegetable stock into a pot and bring to a boil over high heat. Squeeze the cooked garlic out of the skin onto a work surface, discarding the skin and root portion. Reduce the heat to medium-low so the liquid simmers and stir in the cooked tomatoes, shallots, and garlic. Add the 6 basil leaves, remaining ¼ cup olive oil, and the crème fraîche. Working in batches, if necessary, carefully transfer the hot soup to a blender and puree until smooth. Return the soup to a clean pot and reheat if necessary.

To serve, divide the soup among serving bowls and garnish with a touch of sea salt, a drizzle of olive oil, and a few basil leaves.

CLASSIC BEAUJOLAIS

Chinese Chicken Salad

MAKES 4 TO 6 SERVINGS

Throughout the years, Cafe Beaujolais has always had a Chinese chicken salad on the lunch menu. It is a recipe that has its roots going back to the era of Margaret Fox. Many of the recipes from back in those days have lost their luster due to the constant change in people's palates and food trends, but I believe this recipe still has relevance and a sense of nostalgia. Give this recipe a shot and let your taste buds and imagination take you back to the 1980s.

VINAIGRETTE

- 1 cup sweet chili sauce
- ⅔ cup unseasoned rice vinegar
- Juice of 2 limes
- 3 tablespoons mirin
- 2 tablespoons finely diced pickled ginger
- 2 tablespoons soy sauce
- 1 tablespoon toasted sesame oil
- 2 teaspoons fish sauce
- 3 tablespoons brown sugar
- 2 makrut lime leaves
- 1 cup grapeseed oil or olive oil
- Fine sea salt

SALAD

- 4 boneless, skinless chicken breasts, butterflied
- Grapeseed oil
- 1 head napa cabbage, thinly sliced
- ½ head red cabbage, thinly sliced
- 2 cups mixed salad greens
- 1 large carrot, cut into julienne
- 2 oranges, segmented
- 1 red bell pepper, cut into julienne
- ½ cup toasted pine nuts
- Leaves from several sprigs fresh cilantro
- 1 cup purchased crispy noodles
- 1 bunch green onions, trimmed and sliced on the diagonal

To make the vinaigrette, combine the chili sauce, rice vinegar, lime juice, mirin, pickled ginger, soy sauce, sesame oil, fish sauce, brown sugar, and lime leaves in a blender. Blend on high until the ingredients are well mixed. Turn the blender to medium-low speed and slowly drizzle the oil through the hole in the top of the blender until emulsified. Taste, adjusting the seasoning with salt, if needed. Set aside.

To make the salad, place a cast-iron grill on the stove top over high heat. Turn on your kitchen ventilation. Place the chicken breasts onto a plate and drizzle with grapeseed oil and sprinkle lightly with salt. When the pan is smoking, carefully place the chicken on the hot pan. Cook until the chicken is well marked with grill marks and cooked through, about 4 minutes on each side. Transfer to a plate to rest for at least 5 minutes. Cut the chicken crosswise into slices.

When ready to serve, add the red and green cabbage and mixed greens to a large salad bowl. Add dressing to taste and toss to coat the greens well. Add the sliced chicken, toss briefly, then divide the salad among serving plates. Garnish each salad with some carrot, orange segments, bell pepper, pine nuts, cilantro, crispy noodles, and green onions. Serve right away.

Original Cafe Beaujolais Black Bean Chili

CLASSIC BEAUJOLAIS

Surely no old-time Cafe Beaujolais preparation is found in more fans' freezers around the country than this one, a stick-to-your-ribs vegetarian chili so satisfying and easy to make. To my amazement, Julia Child ordered this homey dish when she visited the Beaujolais in the mid-1980s. Topped with grated cheese and served with warmed corn tortillas, it was a healthy, economical meal that we wound up making by the boatload for a very long time once word got out about Julia's choice. —MF

MAKES 8 TO 10 SERVINGS

- 2 tablespoons cumin seed
- 2 tablespoons Beaujolais Blend Herbs (page 292)
- ½ cup olive oil
- 2 large yellow onions, finely chopped
- 1½ cups finely chopped green bell peppers
- 2 cloves garlic, minced (optional)
- 1 teaspoon cayenne pepper
- 1½ tablespoons paprika
- 1 teaspoon kosher salt
- 3 cups canned whole tomatoes, crushed
- ½ cup finely chopped jalapeño peppers (canned are fine)
- ½ pound cheddar or Monterey jack cheese, grated
- ⅔ cup sour cream
- ½ cup green onions
- 8 sprigs fresh cilantro (and if you really like cilantro, then 2 tablespoons more to sprinkle on top)

Sort through the beans and remove the funky ones and the small pebbles. (They're always there. Our prep cook didn't like doing it either.) Rinse well. Place the beans in a large pot, and cover with water until it's several inches above the top of the beans. Cover and bring to a boil. Reduce the heat and cook until the beans are tender, about 1¾ hours. You will need to add more water if the water level reduces enough to expose the beans.

When the beans are cooked, reserve 1 cup of cooking water. Drain the beans, then return them to the pot and add back the reserved cooking water.

Place the cumin seed and Beaujolais Blend Herbs in a small pan and bake in a 325°F oven for 10 to 12 minutes until the fragrance is toasty.

In a skillet over medium heat, warm the oil and sauté the onions, green peppers, and garlic the with cumin seeds and herbs, cayenne pepper, paprika, and salt, until onions are soft, about 10 minutes. Add the tomatoes and jalapeños. Transfer this mixture to the beans and stir well.

To serve, place 1 ounce grated cheese, then 1¼ cups hot chili in a heated bowl. Place a spoonful of sour cream on top. Sprinkle with 1 tablespoon green onions and place a sprig of cilantro or about ½ teaspoon chopped cilantro on the sour cream. Serve warm.

MODERN BEAUJOLAIS

Julian's Black Bean Soup

MAKES 6 SERVINGS

CHIPOTLE CREMA

1 cup sour cream

1 tablespoon adobo sauce (from the chipotle in adobo can for the soup below)

Juice of 1 lime

1 teaspoon fine sea salt

BLACK BEAN SOUP

1 tablespoon extra-virgin olive oil

2 yellow onions, finely diced

4 cloves garlic, minced

1 tablespoon Dutch process cocoa powder

1 teaspoon paprika

1 teaspoon cumin seed, toasted and ground

½ teaspoon ground cinnamon

2 tablespoons tomato paste

2 chipotle chiles in adobo, finely chopped

2 red bell peppers, charred, peeled, and diced

4 cups dried black beans, picked over, then soaked overnight and drained

6 cups low-sodium vegetable broth

2 bay leaves

1 tablespoon fine sea salt

Crumbled queso fresco, for serving

Chopped fresh cilantro, for serving

Grilled sourdough bread, for serving

One of the more famous stories in the fifty-five plus years of Cafe Beaujolais's history involves a bowl of chili. The world-famous Julia Child traveled to the cafe to eat lunch. On that day back in the 1980s, she ordered the black bean chili and proceeded to write about it in San Francisco's newspaper, the Chronicle. *Following the publication of the article, troves of foodies from the Bay Area made the trip up to Mendocino in order to get their fill of that hearty bowl of beans. We still serve the original version on our menu during the winter months in order to pay homage to Margaret's recipe (see page 103). Delicious as the original chili is, I have created my own interpretation featuring a bit more spice and some cocoa powder for depth. I also top it with a chipotle crema for a smoky-creamy finishing note.*

To make the crema, in a bowl, mix together the sour cream, adobo sauce, lime juice, and salt. Cover and refrigerate until ready to serve to blend the flavors.

To make the soup, place a Dutch oven or large stock pot over medium heat. Add the olive oil and onions and sauté until translucent, 8 to 10 minutes. Add the garlic and cook until fragrant, about 1 minute. Add the cocoa powder, paprika, cumin, cinnamon, and tomato paste and cook, stirring, to take the edge off the rawness of the spices, about 1 minute. Add the chopped chipotle chiles and bell pepper. Add the drained black beans, vegetable broth, bay leaves, and salt. Bring to a simmer and turn the heat to low. Cook until the black beans are tender and the soup is full flavored, adding water if needed to keep the beans submerged, 45 to 60 minutes.

To serve, divide the soup among serving bowls. Top with queso fresco, cilantro, and a healthy scoop of the chipotle crema. Serve warm accompanied by grilled sourdough bread.

Clam Chowder

CLASSIC
BEAUJOLAIS

This recipe turned me into a devotee of clam chowder. My prior experience with thick, flour-based versions had left me unimpressed. But this lighter rendition is a perfect match for our foggy coastal clime. —MF

MAKES 6 SERVINGS

- 4 slices bacon, coarsely chopped
- 3 green onions, minced
- 1½ pounds red potatoes, unpeeled, cut into ½-inch cubes
- ½ cup finely chopped green or red bell pepper, or a mixture
- ½ cup finely chopped celery
- 1 tablespoon minced garlic
- 1 cup cold water
- 1 cup clam juice
- 1 teaspoon kosher salt
- ½ teaspoon ground white pepper
- 1 teaspoon Worcestershire sauce
- 2 drops Tabasco sauce or 1 pinch cayenne pepper
- 1 cup frozen corn kernels (do not defrost)
- 3 (6½ ounce) cans clams, with juice
- 2 cups half-and-half

In a large pot over medium-low heat, sauté the bacon until crisp. Set aside. Discard half the fat from the pot. To the pot, add the onions, potatoes, bell pepper, celery, garlic, water, clam juice, salt, pepper, Worcestershire sauce, and Tabasco or cayenne pepper. Bring to a simmer, cover, and simmer until the potatoes are tender, about 15 minutes. Stir in the corn.

Into another pan, pour the clams with their juice and gently warm over medium-low heat until just warmed through, about 5 minutes. Add the warmed clams to the pot, along with the half-and-half. Warm through gently; do not boil.

To serve, divide the chowder among soup bowls and serve right away.

MODERN
BEAUJOLAIS

Chipotle Seafood Chowder

MAKES 4 SERVINGS

1 tablespoon grapeseed oil

4 ears fresh corn, husks removed

6 cups half-and-half

6 tablespoons unsalted butter

4 shallots, finely chopped

3 cloves garlic, minced

1 tablespoon fine sea salt

1 tablespoon Spanish smoked paprika

1 tablespoon ground chipotle powder

2 dried morita chiles

2 tablespoons all-purpose flour

4 stalks celery, chopped

10 fingerling potatoes, cut into ½-inch pieces

10 white shrimp, peeled, deveined, and chopped

2 cups chopped shelled clams

Chopped fresh cilantro, for serving

Crusty sourdough bread, for serving

It's hard to impress me with traditional clam or seafood chowders. In my opinion, many chowders tend to be basic, creamy, pedestrian vessels for whatever seafood may be added to them. In this recipe I wanted to spice up the traditional interpretation and give chowder a new twist. This recipe calls for shrimp and clams, but the creamy base of this recipe works for any type of seafood. I have used crab, local rock cod, and even octopus. Let your imagination run wild and use your own favorite fish or seafood in this flavor-packed version.

Warm a cast-iron skillet over high heat. Turn on your kitchen ventilation. Once the pan is fully heated, add the grapeseed oil and swirl to coat the bottom. Place the corn ears into the pan. Carefully char the corn, turning as needed, until the cobs are evenly browned, about 6 minutes. Turn off the heat and transfer the corn to a clean plate or rack to cool completely. Using a large, sharp knife, remove the kernels from the charred corn cobs and set aside.

Pour the half-and-half in a small saucepan and place over medium heat. Once simmering, remove from the heat and set aside.

Place a large pot or Dutch oven over medium heat. Add the butter, shallots, garlic, and salt and sauté until the shallots are translucent, about 5 minutes. Add the paprika, chipotle powder, and whole dried chiles to the pot. Cook for 1 minute to soften the rawness of the spices. Add the flour and cook for an additional 2 minutes to form a roux. Slowly pour the warm half and half into the pot, whisking to ensure no lumps form. Add the celery and potatoes. Bring the liquid to a simmer and cook until the potatoes are tender, 20 to 30 minutes. Add the chopped shrimp, clams, and charred corn kernels. Cook until the shrimp are tender and just cooked through, 3 to 4 minutes.

Divide the chowder among serving bowls and garnish with chopped cilantro. Serve with sourdough bread.

Summer Greek Salad

This recipe is a simple summer delight. It's an easy way to use up the delicious vegetables that pop up during the summertime. I love serving this in the Beaujolais garden and believe it to be one of the better pizza accompaniments. I find the brightness of the fresh mint and tangy vinaigrette a refreshing reprieve from the summer sun.

MAKES 2 SERVINGS

DRESSING

½ cup extra-virgin olive oil

⅓ cup red wine vinegar

2 cloves garlic, minced

1 teaspoon dried Greek oregano

1 teaspoon Dijon mustard

1 teaspoon fine sea salt

½ teaspoon freshly cracked black pepper

2 cucumbers

1 pint cherry tomatoes

1 cup cooked red quinoa, drained and cooled

4 ounces good-quality feta cheese

½ cup loosely packed whole mint leaves

To make the dressing, combine the oil, vinegar, garlic, oregano, mustard, salt, and pepper in a blender and blend until emulsified.

Quarter the cucumbers and cut them into ¼-inch pieces. Stem and halve the cherry tomatoes.

In a bowl, combine the cucumbers, tomatoes, and quinoa. Crumble the feta cheese over the top and add the mint leaves. Pour the dressing over the salad and toss well. Divide among serving plates and serve right away.

Spaghetti Carbonara

MAKES 4 SERVINGS

- 8 local, farm-fresh or organic egg yolks, at room temperature
- ½ cup plus 1 teaspoon fine sea salt
- 1 teaspoon freshly cracked black pepper, plus more for serving
- ½ cup grated pecorino Romano cheese, plus more for serving
- 1 cup cubed guanciale (¼ inch cubes)
- 1 tablespoon butter
- 1 pound semolina spaghetti

I learned how to make carbonara while I was working in Civitavecchia, a small town located outside Rome in the state of Lazio. While there, I began to understand that the beauty of Italian cooking is its focus on simplicity. Carbonara is a perfect example of this simplicity, consisting of just five ingredients. You'll want to seek out good guanciale, Italian-style cured pork jowl. In my opinion, there is no substitute to the flavor that the guanciale adds to the dish. I do not recommend substituting pancetta, which is what many recipes call for. You can find guanciale in a well-stocked butcher shop, upscale food market, or through an online source.

Bring a large pot of water to a boil over high heat.

In a large bowl, combine the egg yolks, 1 teaspoon salt, pepper, and grated pecorino and whisk until a paste is formed. Set aside.

In a large sauté pan, combine the guanciale and butter and place over medium-low heat. Cook the guanciale until the fat melts and starts to brown slightly, about 4 minutes. Remove the pan from the heat and set aside to cool slightly.

Add the ½ cup salt to the pasta water and return it to a boil. Add the spaghetti to the water and cook until al dente, following the instructions on the package.

A minute before the pasta is cooked, scoop out ½ cup of the pasta water from the pot, and add it to the egg mixture while whisking vigorously (this helps "temper" the egg yolks so that they won't overcook).

Drain the spaghetti, being sure to drain every last drop of water. Add the hot spaghetti to the pan with the guanciale and use tongs to stir well, making sure each pasta strand is coated with the rendered fat from the guanciale. Working quickly, use a rubber spatula to scrape the egg mixture directly into the sauté pan with the pasta. Mix thoroughly, again trying to ensure that each pasta strand is coated.

Immediately divide the spaghetti among serving bowls (warmed bowls is preferable). Sprinkle servings with grated pecorino Romano and cracked black pepper and serve right away.

Pasta Norcina

This is a classic Italian recipe for pasta in sausage cream sauce. In the U.S., it's common to think of sausage as a ground meat and fat mixture stuffed into a casing, generally the intestine of the animal. But at Beaujolais, the majority of sausage we make is considered "bulk" sausage, or sausage without a casing, as is common in the central Umbria region of Italy. There are three main techniques to create this recipe: Cooking the sausage over low heat to render the fat and meld the spices; fully cooking the mushrooms to remove as much liquid content as possible; and cooking the pasta until three-fourths cooked in boiling salted water and then finishing cooking it in the sauce–this allows the natural starch in the pasta to thicken the sauce a bit.

MAKES 4 SERVINGS

SAUSAGE

4 cloves garlic, crushed

1 tablespoon fresh marjoram leaves

1 tablespoon fresh sage leaves

1 tablespoon fresh thyme leaves

1 bay leaf

1 tablespoon sugar

1 teaspoon fine sea salt

1 tablespoon black peppercorns, roughly cracked

1 pound ground pork shoulder

1 pound wild mushrooms, such as porcini, hedgehogs, yellow chanterelles, or cremini, cleaned and chopped

2 tablespoons high-smoke-point oil, such as grapeseed

½ cup Marsala wine

½ cup heavy whipping cream

Fine sea salt and freshly ground black pepper

½ cup unsalted butter, cut into ½-inch cubes

1 pound rigatoni

Freshly grated Parmigiano-Reggiano cheese, for serving

To make the sausage, in a food processor, combine the garlic, marjoram, sage, thyme, bay leaf, sugar, salt, and pepper. Blend until a paste forms. Transfer the herb mixture to a bowl along with the ground pork. Gently fold the ingredients with a wooden spoon until incorporated, taking care not to overmix.

Bring a large pot of generously salted water to a boil over high heat. (A general guideline for cooking pasta is that the water should taste like sea water. Usually, if I am using roughly 8 quarts of water, I add ¼ cup of sea salt.)

Warm a heavy-bottomed skillet over high heat. When the pan is smoking, add the mushrooms (there's no need to add oil at this point). You will begin to see water sweat out of the mushrooms. Cook without stirring for 1 minute, then add the oil. Sauté the mushrooms until golden brown, 3 to 4 minutes. Transfer the mushrooms to a paper towel–lined plate to drain.

CONTINUED

Pasta Norcina *(continued)*

Warm a heavy-bottomed skillet over medium heat. When hot, add the sausage mixture and use a wooden spoon to break up the mixture with a wooden spoon to spread it out in the pan as much as you can. Cook the pork, stirring it occasionally and spreading it back out until you begin to see crispy browned bits forming on the ground pork, 10 to 15 minutes. As you cook, you will see steam forming—this is a good sign that the fat is rendering as it should.

Using caution, add the marsala to the pan. TAKE NOTE: this may cause a flame to shoot up out of the pan, but do not be alarmed! This is just the alcohol of the wine dissipating. Cook until the wine has evaporated nearly dry, about 2 minutes. Add the cream and continue to cook until the mixture is reduced by half, about 2 minutes. Add the cooked mushrooms and stir to incorporate. Taste the sauce and adjust the seasonings with salt and pepper. Set the pan aside.

Add the rigatoni to the boiling water and cook for 2 minutes fewer than the package instructions. (For example, if the package says it takes 12 minutes to cook, cook it for 10).

At the 9 minute mark, reheat the sausage-mushroom mixture until simmering. Scoop out 1 cup of the pasta cooking water. Drain the rigatoni and add to the sausage-mushroom mixture along with the pasta water. Cook, stirring until the pasta is al dente, and the sauce coats it well, 3 to 4 minutes.

Divide the pasta among shallow bowls and sprinkle servings generously with cheese. Serve hot.

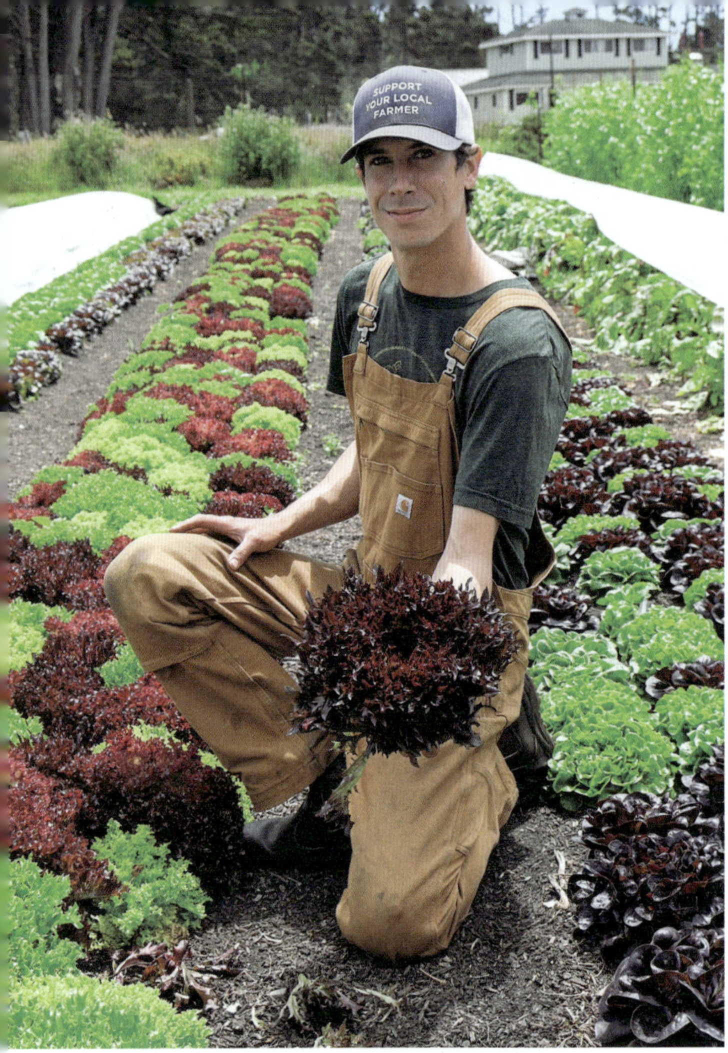
SUPPORT
YOUR LOCAL
FARMER

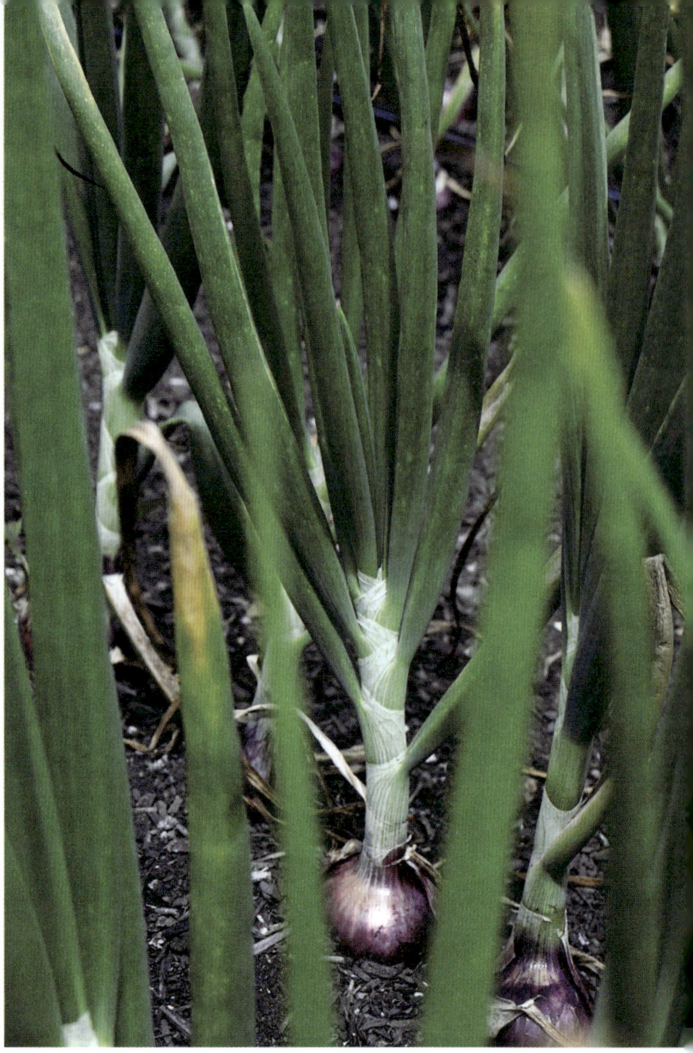

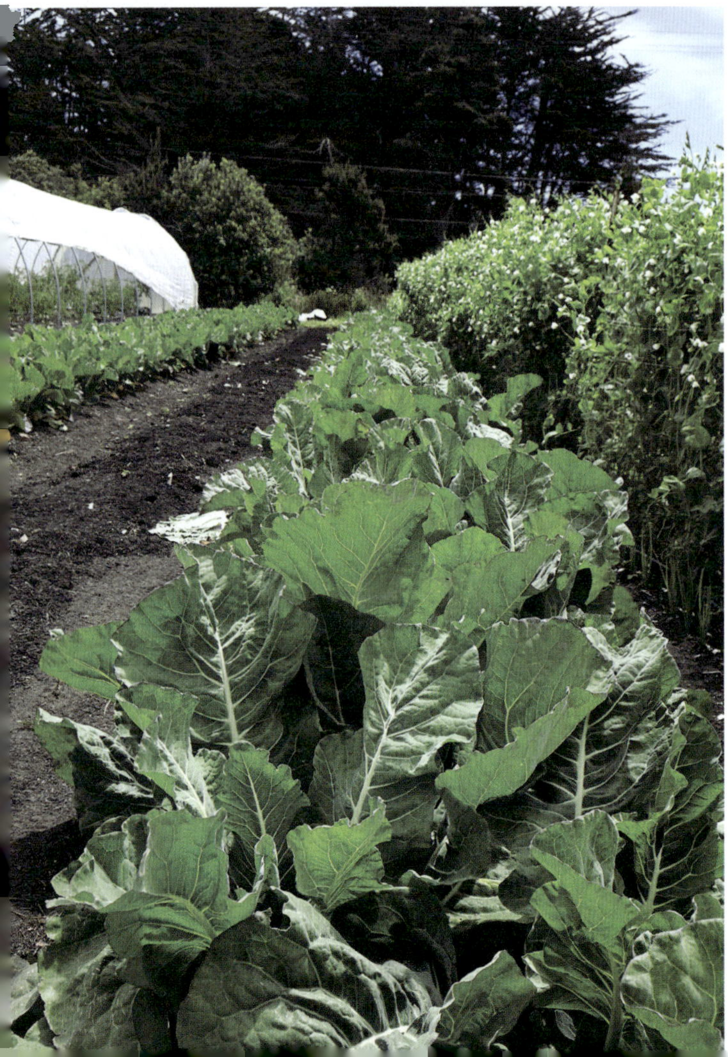

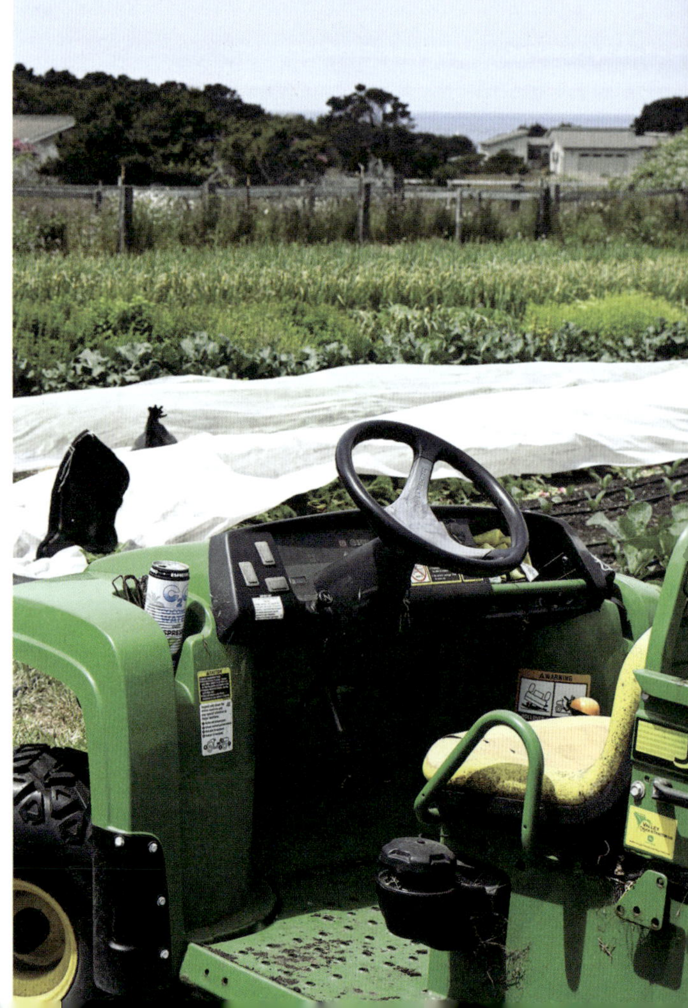

SUPPLIER SPOTLIGHT

Nye Ranch

In 2015, just a year before I arrived at Cafe Beaujolais, Kyle and Mel Burns began transforming Nye Ranch into the bountiful farm it is today. Situated a mere 1,200 feet from the Pacific Ocean, the ranch is located on the stunning rugged coast by MacKerricher State Park in Fort Bragg, a 15 minute drive up the coast. The Ranch grows delicious, sustainable produce for the Mendocino community that works in harmony with the soil and the sea. Kyle and Mel's dedication to harnessing the unique foggy maritime climate yields outstanding crops and effectively puts a new generation of farmers on the local map. Kyle's younger brother, Shea, now runs the farm with his partner, Blair, carrying on their predecessors' strong ethos and continuing their consistent quality.

At Cafe Beaujolais, we value Nye Ranch's dish-defining produce that enhances both our menu and our community. Their greens, brassicas, and root vegetables thrive in our coastal climate, and their delectable tomatoes grow throughout a long and cool season from June to November. We're also obsessed with Nye's purple daikon radishes and flavorful beets. Our friends at Nye Ranch grow the proverbial rainbow from strawberries, squash, and sugar snap peas, to sunflowers, snapdragons, and more.

Our weekly conversations with Kyle and now Shea have continually brought extraordinary color and inspiration to Cafe Beaujolais's seasonally focused menus. Shea thoughtfully solicits our produce wish list, then plants those seeds, and when he walks in the kitchen door a few months later with bunches of our requested Tokyo turnips, for example, our culinary imaginations go wild. Then there was the game-changing spring day when Kyle showed up at the restaurant with a whole load of freshly harvested garlic scapes from their large heirloom garlic crop. It was a revelatory discovery for our team that's since become a seasonal mainstay in our culinary repertoire. We have great fun incorporating the long green shoots in everything from scones to duck breasts and playing with their texture by flash-frying them for instant satisfaction and pickling them so they'll last long beyond the short three-week growing window.

We're truly blessed to have the wonderful folks at Nye Ranch and their high-quality crops so near to us. Not every restaurant can ask their farmer to harvest an order in a pinch and then jet over to the cafe mid-service.

Get your hands on Nye Ranch's fruits, veggies, and flowers at their farmstand off Highway 1 on Saturdays or at the Fort Bragg farmers' market on Wednesdays, and then recreate a Beaujolais salad with some of the very best produce in town!

Pizza Dough

MAKES DOUGH FOR 6 OR 7 PIZZAS

- 1⅔ teaspoons (5 grams) active dry yeast
- 2½ cups (600 grams) warm water (about 110°F)
- 3½ cups (500 grams) 00 flour
- 3½ cups (500 grams) high-protein flour
- 2 tablespoons (30 grams) fine sea salt
- 1½ tablespoons (20 grams) extra-virgin olive oil

At The Brickery, we serve hundreds of pizzas per day and have dialed in our dough recipe. This pizza dough recipe along with our wood-fired oven is the key to our pizza's delicious and unique taste. I ran through loads of different recipes to try and translate the uniqueness that we have created at the restaurant, and I believe I have come close to replicating the actual recipe for the home cook, but just know that the majority of the flavor of our pizza comes from our brick wood-fired bread oven.

With that in mind, there are a few important things to think about with the ingredients listed here. It is extremely important to source the flours listed—substituting flours such as bread flour or all-purpose flour will not create a pizza crust to be proud of. I insist on sourcing a high-quality 00 flour and using a quality high-protein flour. At The Brickery we exclusively use Central Milling Flour, but you can use any reputable brand as long as it is listed as being 00 and high-protein. If you have trouble sourcing these types of flours from your local grocer, try finding them online, as they tend to be readily available.

In a large mixing bowl, whisk the yeast with the warm water until dissolved. Add the flours. Using a wooden spoon, mix until a dough just begins to form; it should not look smooth. Cover the dough well with plastic wrap so that it is airtight. Let rest for 30 minutes. This technique allows the gluten strands to hydrate and strengthen. It also builds up the gluten in the dough without having to aggressively knead it.

CONTINUED

Pizza Dough *(continued)*

Once 30 minutes have passed, sprinkle the salt and olive oil over the dough. Remove the dough from the bowl and place it on a wooden work surface. Knead the dough until it is smooth and elastic, 10 to 15 minutes. Wrap the kneaded dough tightly with a plastic bag or plastic wrap, making sure it's in an airtight environment so that the dough doesn't create a crust and dry out. Let rest at room temperature (in a spot that is not too cold) until the dough has doubled in size, about 1 hour, this technique is called the bench rest.

Using a bench scraper, portion the dough into 6 or 7 evenly shaped circular balls. If you have a scale in your kitchen the ideal weight is 250 grams or roughly 9 ounces. Place the balls into an oiled container with a lid and place the lid on top. Let the dough balls stand at room temperature for 30 minutes (they will rise slightly) and then place the dough in the refrigerator for a minimum of 12 hours, or preferably 24 to 36 hours, being sure the container is airtight. The dough will keep for up to 48 hours in the refrigerator before baking.

About 2 hours before baking, remove the dough ball(s) from the refrigerator. It's important to allow the dough to come to room temperature. Room-temperature dough is easier to stretch and bakes more evenly.

You can freeze the portioned dough balls in an airtight container for up to 1 month. The day before you want to make pizza, remove the dough from the freezer and let it thaw in the refrigerator. When ready to bake, let the dough come to room temperature, up to 4 hours, depending on the temperature of the room.

Vietnamese Pizza

My love for Vietnamese food is beyond description—so much so that one day I decided to try my hand at incorporating Vietnamese flavors into a pizza. Pizza purists might balk at this—and when I first put this pizza on my menu at The Brickery not a single coworker or customer thought it would work. Little did they know, the pizza would become one of our most successful sellers. The salty, oily dough is a perfect vessel to allow the funky, tangy Vietnamese flavors shine. Try it out and let your taste buds sing. The pesto freezes really well and can be used to flavor many different things, such as pasta, fish, or shrimp.

MAKES 1 PIZZA

VIETNAMESE PESTO

1 lemongrass stalk, outer layers removed, crushed and chopped

6 cloves garlic

1 shallot, chopped

1-inch knob ginger, peeled and chopped

2 tablespoons fish sauce

2 tablespoons sugar

½ cup fresh lime juice

1 tablespoon rice vinegar

1 tablespoon red pepper flakes

1 teaspoon fine sea salt

4 cups fresh spinach

Leaves from 1 bunch Thai basil

Leaves from 1 bunch fresh mint

Leaves and stems from 1 bunch fresh cilantro

Leaves from 1 bunch fresh shiso

1½ cups olive oil

PIZZA

1 ball Pizza Dough (page 120), at room temperature

1 cup shredded low-moisture mozzarella cheese

¼ cup grated Parmigiano-Reggiano cheese

½ cup shredded Duck Confit (page 194)

¼ cup sliced Pickled Fresno Chiles (page 293)

Small handful each of fresh Thai basil, mint, cilantro and shiso leaves

1 lime

Preheat the oven to 550°F or as high as your oven will go. Place a pizza stone into the oven to preheat.

To make the pesto, in a food processor, combine the lemongrass, garlic, shallot, ginger, fish sauce, sugar, lime juice, vinegar, red pepper flakes, and salt. Pulse until a smooth paste forms. Using a rubber spatula, scrape the paste into a bowl and set aside. Add the spinach, basil, mint, cilantro, and shiso to the food processor. With the machine running, slowly drizzle the oil until a smooth paste forms. Scrape this paste into the bowl with the lemongrass mixture and fold together until well mixed.

Put the pizza dough ball onto a lightly floured work surface. Flatten the dough and stretch it, using your hands and gravity, into a 12-inch round. Transfer the dough round to a pizza peel lightly dusted with flour.

Spread an even layer of the pesto onto the dough, using about ¾ cup. (Reserve the remaining pesto for another pizza, or another use). Top with shredded mozzarella, grated Parmesan, duck confit, and Fresno chiles. Slide the pizza onto the pizza stone and cook until the cheese is melted and the toppings are bubbling, or until done to your liking, 6 to 10 minutes.

Using the pizza peel, remove the pizza from the oven and slide it onto a cutting board. Top it with the basil, mint, cilantro, shiso, and a healthy squeeze of lime juice. Cut the pizza into wedges and serve right away.

Wild Mushroom Pizza

MAKES 1 PIZZA

- 1 pound wild mushrooms, such as chanterelles and morels, cleaned
- 1 teaspoon fine sea salt
- 2 tablespoons unsalted butter
- 1 clove garlic, crushed
- 1 sprig fresh thyme
- ½ teaspoon freshly cracked black pepper
- 1 ball Pizza Dough (page 120), at room temperature
- ½ cup crème fraîche
- ½ cup shredded low-moisture mozzarella cheese
- ¼ cup grated pecorino Romano cheese, plus more for sprinkling

When wild mushroom season rolls around in the Mendocino region, this pizza immediately becomes the number one seller at The Brickery. People are obsessed with the idea of eating a product whose ingredients are foraged minutes away from where they are eating. I find that fresh crispy dough, tangy cheese, and earthy wild mushrooms are one of the world's great pleasures.

Preheat the oven to 550°F or as high as your oven will go. Place a pizza stone into the oven to preheat.

Place a cast-iron skillet over high heat. Working in batches if necessary to avoid crowding the pan, add the mushrooms and salt to the hot skillet and cook, stirring every minute or so, until the mushrooms begin taking on some color and have released their liquid, 4 to 6 minutes. Remove the pan from the heat and add the butter, garlic, thyme, and pepper and stir to combine.

Put the pizza dough ball onto a lightly floured work surface. Flatten the dough and stretch it, using your hands and gravity, into a 12-inch round. Transfer the dough round to a pizza peel lightly dusted with flour.

Evenly spread the crème fraîche over the pizza dough round. Sprinkle evenly with the mozzarella and pecorino, then top with the cooked mushroom mixture. Slide the pizza onto the pizza stone and cook until the cheese is melted and the toppings are bubbling, or until done to your liking, 6 to 10 minutes.

Using the pizza peel, remove the pizza from the oven and slide it onto a cutting board. Top it with additional grated pecorino. Cut the pizza into wedges and serve right away.

WAITING
ROOM

Fennel Sausage Pizza

MAKES 1 PIZZA

SAUSAGE

1 tablespoon whole fennel seeds

1 tablespoon sugar

1 teaspoon fine sea salt

1 teaspoon red pepper flakes

1 teaspoon dried oregano

4 cloves garlic, minced

1 pound ground pork

1 ball Pizza Dough (page 120), at room temperature

¾ cup Bianco di Napoli whole tomatoes, crushed by hand or with an immersion blender

¾ cup shredded mozzarella cheese (Grande brand is best)

¼ red onion, thinly sliced, or to taste

2 tablespoons cured pitted black olives, or to taste

2 tablespoons Pickled Fresno Chiles (page 293), or to taste

This was the first pizza sold at The Brickery and it is one that will never leave our menu. We have many locals that frequent The Brickery weekly for their sausage pizza fix. I think pizzas with meat need balance and the formula to create balance is to blend salty, sweet, tangy, spicy, and fatty flavors. In this recipe the black olives provide the salt; the pickled Fresno chiles provide the tangy and spice; the cheese and sausage provide the fat; and the onions provide the sweetness. In my opinion, using homemade sausage is crucial to this pizza's success. Store-bought ground sausage usually contains fillers and sugars that can throw off the balance. Rendering the sausage before placing it on the pizza is also an important step as it adds texture to the final pizza. Crispy, fatty, tangy, salty, sweet—this is pizza perfection.

Preheat the oven to 400°F.

In a small dry sauté pan, toast the fennel seeds over medium heat until lightly toasted, 1 to 2 minutes. Pour them onto a plate to stop the cooking.

In a mini food processor, combine the sugar, salt, red pepper flakes, oregano, garlic, and toasted fennel seeds and process until blended. In a large bowl, using clean hands, gently mix the pork with the spice mixture until blended. Press the mixture onto a rimmed baking sheet in a thin layer. Bake until the sausage is browned and the fat has rendered, 15 to 20 minutes. Remove the sausage from the oven and let cool. Once cooled, crumble the sausage by hand into manageable pieces to use on the pizza. Set aside.

Increase the oven heat to 550°F or as high as your oven will go. Place a pizza stone into the oven to preheat.

Put the pizza dough ball onto a lightly floured work surface. Flatten the dough and stretch it, using your hands and gravity, into a 12-inch round. Transfer the dough round to a pizza peel lightly dusted with flour.

Ladle the crushed tomatoes onto the dough round and spread it out evenly. Evenly sprinkle the shredded mozzarella over the sauce, focusing on spreading the cheese more heavily on the outer rim of the pizza and less in the center. Top evenly with your desired number of onions, olives, Fresno chiles, and crumbled sausage.

Slide the pizza onto the pizza stone and cook until the cheese is melted and the crust is golden brown, or until done to your liking, about 6 to 10 minutes. Using the pizza peel, remove the pizza from the oven and slide it onto a cutting board. Cut the pizza into wedges and serve right away.

Pizza with Spinach-Basil Pesto

MAKES 1 PIZZA

SPINACH-BASIL PESTO

3 cloves garlic, crushed

1 teaspoon red pepper flakes

1 teaspoon fine sea salt

Finely grated zest of 1 lemon

¼ cup blanched slivered almonds

½ cup loosely packed fresh basil leaves

1 cup extra-virgin olive oil

4 cups loosely packed baby spinach

¼ cup fresh lemon juice

PIZZA

1 ball Pizza Dough (page 120), at room temperature

¾ cup grated mozzarella cheese

¼ cup soft goat cheese

1 Lemon Confit (page 292), cut into matchstick strands

½ cup snap peas, cut into diagonal pieces

What most people think of as the original pesto, also known as pesto alla Genovese, is traditionally made with basil, pine nuts, extra-virgin olive oil, crushed garlic, and a generous amount of grated Parmigiano-Reggiano cheese. In this recipe I add spinach to balance the floral notes of the basil, which I find to be a distraction. This substitution adds nutrients, flavor, and a vibrant green color. I think the balance of basil, spinach, and lemon works perfectly with the mozzarella, goat cheese, and snap peas that we use for the pesto pizza. Any leftover pesto can be used for a multitude of things, such as a substitute for mayonnaise in a sandwich, tossing with pasta, or as a topping for grilled chicken breasts.

To make the Spinach-Basil Pesto, in a food processor, combine the garlic, red pepper flakes, salt, lemon zest, almonds, and basil. Process the ingredients until a paste forms. With the machine running, add one-third of the olive oil to loosen the paste. Add about one-third of the spinach and process until smooth. Repeat these steps two more times until you have a solid, yet loose texture. Add the lemon juice and pulse a few more times to mix. (Makes about 3 cups pesto).

Preheat the oven to 550°F or as high as your oven will go. Place a pizza stone into the oven to preheat.

Put the pizza dough ball onto a lightly floured work surface. Flatten the dough and stretch it, using your hands and gravity, into a 12-inch round. Transfer the dough round to a pizza peel lightly dusted with flour.

Using a rubber spatula or the back of a large spoon, spread ¾ cup of the pesto over the pizza dough, leaving a ½-inch border all the way around. Reserve the remaining pesto for another use. Sprinkle the pizza with the grated mozzarella and dot the pizza evenly with teaspoon-size chunks of the goat cheese. Sprinkle the snap peas and lemon confit evenly over the surface.

Slide the pizza onto the pizza stone and cook until the cheese is melted and the crust is golden brown, or until done to your liking, 6 to 10 minutes. Using the pizza peel, remove the pizza from the oven and slide it onto a cutting board. Cut the pizza into wedges and serve right away.

THE
BRICKERY
WAITING
ROOM

Smash Burgers

MAKES 8 BURGERS

SAUTÉED ONIONS

- 2 large yellow onions, diced
- 1 tablespoon grapeseed oil
- 1 teaspoon balsamic vinegar
- ½ teaspoon fine sea salt
- ½ teaspoon freshly ground black pepper
- 1 tablespoon unsalted butter

SPICED AIOLI

- 1 cup mayonnaise
- 2 tablespoons pickle juice
- 2 tablespoons Cajun Bleu Seasoning (page 292)
- 1 tablespoon ketchup

- 16 ounces medium-grind brisket
- 16 ounces medium-grind chuck
- Salt and freshly ground black pepper
- Grapeseed oil
- 8 slices good-quality American cheese
- 8 toasted burger buns
- 2 whole dill pickles, cut into slices
- Sliced ripe tomatoes
- 1 head iceberg lettuce, cored and outer pieces removed

When I took over the kitchen at Cafe Beaujolais, I wanted to create different avenues for customers to enjoy our food. The restaurant hadn't been able to offer quick-and-easy lunch food during its fifty plus years of existence. I sensed an opportunity. I decided to open the side window on Wednesdays and Thursdays to sell sandwiches. The community showed up in droves and a cult following ensued. Many factors contributed to the success of the sandwich window, where we serve smash burgers and chicken sandwiches. I believe the focus on locally sourced ingredients and, for the burgers, grinding the beef daily, contributed to the hype. In this recipe I detail the steps we take each week to create these delectable burgers.

For the beef, I use a 50/50 blend of brisket and chuck and grind it on a medium-large grinder setting. Pro tip: Ask your local butcher to grind it for you fresh and plan to cook it the same day. It is very important to buy whole dill pickles and slice them before serving. In order to achieve a perfect smash burger, I like to use a flat cast-iron griddle. A large cast-iron skillet will also work, but you won't have as much room for the burger patties to spread. At the restaurant, we wrap the burgers in foil. This gives the burger a more "traditional" takeout feel that adds to the charm of these burgers.

To make the onions, place the diced onions in a cast-iron skillet over medium-low heat. Add the oil, vinegar, salt, and pepper and sauté slowly until they are fully translucent and beginning to brown, 15 to 20 minutes. Add the butter and turn off the heat, folding the butter into the onions until melted. Set aside.

To make the aioli, in a bowl, mix together the mayonnaise, pickle juice, Cajun Bleu Seasoning, and ketchup. Set aside in the refrigerator until serving time.

To make the patties, in a bowl, combine the ground brisket and chuck and gently mix together (it is important to gently combine the beef so that the fat does not emulsify with the meat). Divide the mixture into 8 equal portions. Roll each portion into a ball, season with salt and pepper, and set aside on a plate near the stove.

Set a cast-iron griddle on the stove top over high heat and turn on your kitchen ventilation. When the griddle is very hot and smoking, add a teaspoon of grapeseed oil to the griddle and place a ball of meat on top of the oil. Using two large spatulas, one in each hand, smash the ball into a flat, even patty. Repeat with the remaining patties, using 1 teaspoon of oil per patty.

Cook the beef patties until they are about 80 percent cooked on the first side; the top side of the patties will turn a slight brownish-gray color, about 1½ minutes. Then, using one of the spatulas, carefully scrape the patty off the griddle—the bottom will be crusty—and flip it over. Top each patty with 2 tablespoons of the sautéed onions and a slice of American cheese. Cover the patties with a small metal bowl until the cheese melts, about 10 seconds.

Spread about 1 teaspoon aioli on each side of the toasted buns. Arrange 6 to 8 pickle slices on the aioli on the bottom bun and then top with sliced tomatoes. Place the cooked burger patty on the tomatoes and then top with a thick hunk of lettuce. Cover with the bun top. Wrap the burger in foil, which allows the burger and bun to steam and soften. Serve hot.

Nashville-Style Hot Chicken Sandwiches

MAKES 4 SANDWICHES

MARINATED CHICKEN

- 2 cups buttermilk
- ½ cup Crystal brand hot sauce
- 2 teaspoons cayenne pepper
- 1 tablespoon fine sea salt
- 4 large boneless, skinless chicken thighs

SAUCE

- ½ cup mayonnaise
- 1 tablespoon yellow mustard
- 1 tablespoon honey

- ½ cup instant dried polenta or semolina
- ½ cup tapioca starch
- ½ cup rice flour
- About 2¼ cups peanut oil, or as needed
- ¼ cup cayenne pepper
- ¼ cup chili powder
- ¼ cup honey
- ¼ cup butter, melted, plus 1 tablespoon butter for toasting the buns
- 1 tablespoon fine sea salt
- 4 brioche or challah buns
- 4 pieces iceberg lettuce
- 20 pieces sliced dill pickle

This chicken sandwich started as a special at our takeout window. Customers continually asked for a chicken sandwich to enjoy alongside their smash burgers. Many fried chicken sandwiches use chicken breasts, which I find can be bland. I decided to go with the more flavorful chicken thighs for my sandwich and then doubled down by marinating them in buttermilk for a minimum of 12 hours. A great thing about this recipe is that the cayenne and hot sauce can be omitted if you enjoy the milder side of life. The breading for this chicken is influenced by the Japanese- and Korean-style fried chicken that I discovered while traveling in Asia. The tapioca starch and rice flour allow the chicken to crisp up more than just plain wheat flour and help maintain a crisp texture after being dunked in the flavorful hot sauce. You'll want to plan ahead, as the chicken needs to marinate overnight before cooking.

To marinate the chicken, in a small bowl, mix together the buttermilk, hot sauce, cayenne, and salt. Place the chicken in a gallon-sized locking plastic bag or a container with a lid. Pour the buttermilk mixture over the chicken. Stir the chicken and marinade to ensure the marinade is in contact with every part of the chicken. Seal the bag and refrigerate overnight for at least 12 hours and up to 2 days.

To make the sauce, stir together the mayonnaise, mustard, and honey until well blended. Cover and refrigerate until ready to use.

The next day, in a bowl, mix together the polenta, tapioca starch, and rice flour. Set aside. In another bowl, combine ¼ cup of the peanut oil, the cayenne pepper, chili powder, honey, melted butter, and salt until a stiff paste forms. Set aside.

Place a skillet over medium heat and add 1 tablespoon butter. When the butter melts, add the buns, cut side down, and cook until the buns are golden brown. Remove the buns from the pan and set aside.

Pour the remaining 2 cups oil into a heavy saucepan and place over medium heat. When the oil registers 375°F on a deep-frying thermometer, it is ready for frying. Using tongs, remove the chicken thighs from the marinade, shaking off the excess, and drop into the bowl with the polenta mixture. Turn the chicken thighs in the mixture to ensure each thigh is fully covered. Carefully lower the dredged chicken into the hot oil and cook until dark golden brown, about 5 minutes. Using tongs, remove the chicken thighs from the hot oil, letting the oil drip into the pan for a few seconds, then immediately transfer it to the bowl of chile paste. Use a spoon to scoop the paste over the chicken, being sure that every bit of the crispy chicken is coated with the paste.

Spread both of the cut sides of the buns with a generous tablespoon of the honey-mustard-mayo sauce. For each sandwich, layer 5 pickle slices on the bottom bun, then top with a piece of crispy hot chicken. Place a lettuce leaf atop the chicken and cover with the top bun. Serve right away.

Evening Food

EVENING FOOD

I first visited Cafe Beaujolais on a cold, rainy, February night in 2016. It was my first proper stop in Mendocino. Per my father's insistence, I made a dinner reservation at the restaurant as due diligence to decide if we would buy this once-iconic forty-eight-year-old restaurant. So, on that particular evening, I walked from my hotel down the dark, quiet street, a biting chill penetrating me with every heavy raindrop and gust of coastal wind. But as I approached the old country house at 961 Ukiah Street, a beacon of light beamed through the fog. The warm lights inside Cafe Beaujolais contrasted with the night sky and I could see that the charming dining room was buzzing. Intrigued, I suddenly felt the potential of this curiously mesmerizing and unexpected scene. As I sat in the seemingly ordinary dining room chair, an unforgettable feeling of coziness swept over me. The classic ambiance, the old wood, and a palpable feeling in the air transported me; I was at total ease, completely present with a singular focus on my dining experience. There was a visceral spark in that moment, and although this small-town institution was foreign to me, I knew that the Beaujolais was calling me to carry on her legacy.

It had been seventeen years since Chef Margaret Fox sold Cafe Beaujolais. The mystique that her husband, Chef Chris Kump, cultivated with its buzzy dinner service was dormant, just waiting for someone to come along and revive it. Coincidentally, Chris was twenty-four like I was when he moved up to Mendocino to take over the restaurant, though he came from the SF Bay Area, while I moved up from LA. It was his job to expand the locals' brunch spot to the evening destination restaurant it would later become. During Chris's time it was the 1980s and the new concept of farm-to-table cooking was in its infancy. Chef Chris excelled in his role, cooking up elegant, high-end food and an experience that made reservations nearly impossible to score. Chris and Margaret's Cafe Beaujolais put little Mendocino on the culinary map.

Since that epic era, Cafe Beaujolais's reputation changed as its ownership turned over a few times. The restaurant's bones were still strong, ripe for new blood and new ideas. And here I was, ambition flooding me on that emotional evening. My excitement about this prospect instantly sprouted; I reflexively began thinking about what my food would look like on the table. And just like that, 500 miles from my stomping grounds in LA's bumping food scene, I was home.

Dinner service was my first focus as the new chef-owner of Cafe Beaujolais. Improving the evening food was the initial step in rebuilding

Cafe Beaujolais's reputation. I was trained to prepare dinner at every restaurant I had cooked, and it was where I felt most comfortable, so I felt well prepared for the task.

Food is primal—at its essence, it's nourishment. My approach to cooking is about making people happy through quality and homeyness. Despite my background in Michelin-starred fine-dining restaurants, I gravitate toward traditional, simple, no-frills dining experiences where quality and deliciousness of the ingredients speak for themselves. My food is flavorful, satisfying, and relatable, not avant-garde or stuffy. Ultimately, the food at Cafe Beaujolais has always been and will continue to be all about comfort, which was the perfect match with my cooking sensibility.

Describing my culinary style, however, is a little less simple. In short, my diversified industry experiences have shaped a unique personal style that doesn't conform to a singular category or cuisine. My first formative cooking experience was while working under James Beard Award–winning Chef Jeremy Hanson in Spokane, Washington. His intentional approaches to sourcing local ingredients and whole-animal butchery will be part of my culinary toolkit forever. Next, a stint in France taught me techniques that form the foundation of how I, and many chefs, cook. While working and traveling in Italy, I picked up the brilliant concepts of simplicity and seasonality. Then back home in California, I gained a transformative confidence and playfulness from mentor Chef Charles Olalia through his trusting leadership and impassioned knowledge. Chef Charles, who's Filipino, introduced me to Southeast Asian flavors and flavor enhancers, expanding my palate to exciting layers of sour, sweetness, heat, and umami. He also encouraged me to experiment with these new-to-me flavors, combining the traditions I had adopted into a unique culinary voice of my own.

When I began traveling again, particularly to Vietnam, I discovered even more new flavors that I've integrated into my culinary repertoire. The ability to play with all of the influences from my training—the U.S. West Coast, Europe, and Asia—is so important to the current Cafe Beaujolais experience. We'll take you to Vietnam for your appetizer, Italy for your mid-course, and France for your main dish (and that's without harmonizing beverages). What's more is that these various cooking styles create a diverse menu that opens the door for guests to come multiple times a week, satisfying cravings for different types of cuisines. It's a joy to share the techniques, ingredients, flavors, and styles I've collected along my ever-evolving culinary journey.

All of the recipes in this chapter are dishes that have appeared on the Cafe Beaujolais menu and that reflect my elegant but approachable cooking style. Moreover, they've been selected and written with the intention of being cooked and enjoyed at home. While many of them are easy to make, we embrace the opportunity in a handful of recipes to walk you through valuable cooking techniques that will help you with your other cooking projects. We've also offered a few "stretch recipes" to up your culinary game when you want to feel like a restaurant chef in your home kitchen. Remember to use quality ingredients, and you'll be cooking up Cafe Beaujolais's fun, comforting, accessible menu in no time!

Ahi Tuna Crostini

MAKES 4 CROSTINI

- 8 ounces sushi-grade ahi tuna loin
- 6 tablespoons extra-virgin olive oil, plus more if needed and for garnish
- 1 sheet nori, toasted and finely chopped
- ½ cup pistachios, toasted (see page 295) and roughly chopped
- 2 tablespoons minced shallot, soaked in a mixture of equal parts ice water and red wine vinegar
- 2 tablespoons chopped fresh chives
- 1 tablespoon sesame seeds, toasted (see page 295), plus more for garnish
- 2 tablespoons fresh lemon juice
- 1 ripe avocado, cut into ¼ inch dice
- 1 recipe Grilled Crostini (page 152)
- 1 teaspoon ABC brand sweet soy sauce, for garnish

In my opinion, ahi is best eaten raw or lightly seared on a hot grill. In the kitchen at Cafe Beaujolais, I highlight this fish over a crostino. When I use the language "sushi grade" tuna, I like to look at a few different qualities in the fish. First is color, it needs to be bright red with a nice oily sheen. Second is that the tuna source labels that it was vacuum sealed or should be consumed within a day or two of being caught. Third is the price: high-quality sushi-grade tuna will unfortunately have a higher price point than subpar sourced tuna. So, if those three thresholds are confirmed then you are good to use this for your crostini.

Place the tuna loin on a clean cutting board. Using a large, sharp knife, cut the tuna into ¼-inch strips. Then, cut the strips into ¼-inch cubes. Drizzle the tuna cubes with 2 tablespoons of the oil. (The oil acts as a lubricant so the fish will not stick to the knife while chopping.) Rocking the knife back and forth across the cutting board, mince the tuna pieces until a rough paste is formed, adding more oil if the tuna begins to stick to the knife.

Transfer the tuna paste to a bowl. Add the chopped nori, pistachios, drained shallot, chives, sesame seeds, remaining ¼ cup of the olive oil, and the lemon juice. Using a large spoon, mix gently but thoroughly. Carefully fold in the diced avocado being careful not to mash them. Set the tuna mixture aside while making the crostini.

To assemble, while the crostini are still warm and the scent of the freshly rubbed garlic is in the air, spread a ½-inch layer of the tuna mixture onto each toast. Slice the toasts in half at an angle and sprinkle with a few toasted sesame seeds. Finish with a nice drizzle of olive oil and the sweet soy sauce.

Steak Tartare Crostini

One of the staples on my menu at Cafe Beaujolais is steak tartare, for which I use lean filet mignon. The traditional French style features a raw egg yolk that creates a silky texture. But my recipe has roots in Italian cuisine and offers acidity and saltiness for a meaty, savory, and tart bite. About an hour before beginning, remove the filet mignon from the refrigerator and let it stand at room temperature; this helps ensure the flavors will pop. Serve with an arugula salad lightly dressed with fresh lemon juice and olive oil and enjoy with a chilled, light red wine.

Many manufacturers of balsamic vinegar add mass-market wine vinegar to standardize their product. I advise checking the labels before purchasing. True balsamic vinegars come from Modena, Italy, and say only "grape must" on the label. These vinegars will cost more than the mass market–produced ones, but a little goes a long way and they will increase the quality of the dish. Unless you are making your own, avoid "balsamic glazes," which are generally wine vinegar reduced down with sugar.

MAKES 4 CROSTINI

- 8 ounces room-temperature filet mignon, cleaned of all fat and silver skin, finely minced (ask your local butcher for the end pieces or scraps of the loin)
- 2 tablespoons Dijon mustard
- 2 teaspoons capers, minced
- 2 tablespoons minced shallots, soaked in a mixture of equal parts ice water and red wine vinegar
- 2 tablespoons chopped fresh chives
- 2 tablespoons chopped fresh flat-leaf parsley
- ¼ cup extra-virgin olive oil
- 2 tablespoons fresh lemon juice
- Grilled Crostini (page 152)
- ¼ cup shaved Parmigiano-Reggiano cheese
- Edible flowers, for garnish (optional)
- Aged balsamic vinegar, for garnish

In a bowl, combine the filet mignon, mustard, capers, drained shallot, chives, parsley, olive oil, and lemon juice and mix until incorporated. Let the mixture stand for 5 minutes to blend the flavors. Meanwhile, prepare the crostini.

To assemble, while the crostini are still warm and the scent of the freshly rubbed garlic is in the air, spread a ½-inch layer of the beef mixture onto each toast. Cut each toast at an angle and arrange on a platter. Garnish each piece with a few slivers of Parmigiano-Reggiano cheese. If desired, garnish with a few edible flowers. Drizzle generously with aged balsamic vinegar.

Fava Bean Toast

MAKES 4 CROSTINI

FAVA BEAN PUREE

2½ pounds fava beans

1 tablespoon fine sea salt

½ teaspoon baking soda

¼ cup extra-virgin olive oil

4 cloves garlic, minced

2 shallots, thinly sliced

2 tablespoons chopped Lemon Confit (page 292) or finely grated lemon zest

Juice of 1 lemon

¼ cup crème fraîche or sour cream

½ cup fresh basil leaves, plus more for garnish

¼ cup fresh mint leaves, plus more for garnish

GOAT CHEESE SPREAD

1 cup good-quality fresh goat cheese, preferably spreadable and not in a log

¼ cup crème fraîche or sour cream

2 tablespoons fresh lemon juice

1 teaspoon fine sea salt

1 teaspoon freshly ground black pepper

GRILLED CROSTINI

4 slices (½ inch thick) sourdough bread

Extra-virgin olive oil

1 to 2 large garlic cloves, peeled and kept whole

During the spring, fava beans can be spotted all over my menu at the cafe. They take a bit of prep, which includes shucking them from the pod, then blanching, then removing the outer skin of the beans, but I believe it's worth every minute. I designed this recipe in order to provide a satisfying vegetarian option for our appetizer menu. It combines creamy tangy goat cheese, fresh herbs, and bright lemon. I recommend making these for dinner party appetizers or as a lunch snack on a warm spring day.

Fill a saucepan three-fourths full of water, set over high heat, and bring to a boil. Meanwhile, shuck the fava beans from their pods, discard the pods, and place the beans in a bowl.

Add 1 tablespoon salt and a ½ teaspoon baking soda to the boiling water. Place a bowl filled with ice water on the counter next to the stove.

Carefully add the beans to the boiling water and boil for 2 minutes. (This technique has two purposes. It cooks the fava beans and also loosens the tough outer skin of the beans.) Use a slotted spoon or spider strainer to transfer the beans from the boiling water to the ice bath. Allow the beans to chill for 2 minutes.

Drain the beans. Using your fingers, remove and discard the outer skin from each bean. You should end up with bright-green fava beans.

To a cold sauté pan, add the olive oil, garlic, shallots, and lemon confit. Place the pan on the burner over medium heat. Cook, stirring occasionally, until the shallot is translucent but not browned, about 5 minutes. Add the lemon juice, crème fraîche, shucked fava beans, basil, and mint and cook just until simmering, 1 to 2 minutes. Immediately remove from the heat.

While the fava bean mixture is still warm, transfer it to a food processor. Pulse the machine about 10 times until the mixture is smooth but not pureed. Transfer to a bowl and set aside. Wash and dry the food processor.

To make the goat cheese spread, in a clean food processor bowl, combine the goat cheese, crème fraîche, lemon juice, salt, and pepper and process until smooth.

To make the crostini, preheat a stovetop grill pan or turn on the broiler. Drizzle the sourdough with olive oil and grill or broil until crisp and golden brown, 1 to 2 minutes per side. Immediately rub the toasts with the garlic clove.

To assemble, spread a generous spoonful of the goat cheese mixture onto the toasts, as you would spread cream cheese on a bagel. Top each toast with a large spoonful of the fava bean puree. Arrange the toasts on a platter and garnish with basil and mint leaves. Serve right away.

Crab Cakes, Southeast Asian Style

MAKES 8 TO 10 CRAB CAKES

Three (13.5-ounce) cans unsweetened coconut milk

1 pound cooked Dungeness crabmeat, picked over for cartilage or shells, or any comparable freshly harvested lump crabmeat

3 cloves garlic, minced

2 fresh Thai chiles or red Fresno chiles, finely chopped

1 shallot, minced

1 lemongrass stalk, crushed and finely chopped

2 tablespoons peeled and finely chopped fresh ginger or galangal

2 tablespoons Vietnamese fish sauce, preferably Red Boat brand

1 tablespoon unseasoned rice vinegar

Juice of 1 lime

2 cups panko breadcrumbs

½ cup chopped fresh cilantro

½ cup fresh mint ribbons

½ cup Thai basil or Italian basil leaves

½ cup shiso ribbons (optional)

1 cup high-smoke-point oil, such as grapeseed oil

Sweet and delicate Dungeness crab is a staple along the Northern California Coast from December to March. Restaurants up and down the coast have developed different ways to highlight the prized crustacean, but many restaurants form it into crab cakes. At Beaujolais, we have experimented with many different styles of crab cakes, but our favorite uses Southeast Asian flavors. For this recipe to shine, be sure to use the freshest lump crab meat. Serve the crab cakes alongside an herb salad or with Southern Indian Coconut Rice (page 235).

Pour the coconut milk into a saucepan and place over medium heat. Cook the coconut milk until reduced by three-fourths and the mixture begins to turn a golden-yellow color, 10 to 15 minutes. You should end up with around ¾ cup of liquid. Transfer the mixture to a bowl and place it in the refrigerator to cool.

Meanwhile, in a bowl, combine the crabmeat, garlic, chiles, shallot, lemongrass, ginger, fish sauce, vinegar, and lime juice. Once the coconut milk mixture has cooled slightly, add ½ cup to the crab mixture and gently fold the ingredients together, taking care not to break up the large pieces of crabmeat. Place the mixture in the refrigerator for a minimum of 1 hour and up to 4 hours to firm up. Refrigerate the remaining coconut milk mixture as well.

Remove the crab mixture from the refrigerator and add 1 cup of the panko, the cilantro, mint, basil, and shiso, if using. Gently fold the mixture together until well mixed, again, taking care not to break up the large pieces of crabmeat.

Pour the remaining 1 cup panko into a small bowl. Line a rimmed baking sheet with parchment paper. Using a ⅓ cup measuring cup, scoop up the crab mixture to form evenly shaped crab cakes and transfer them to the lined baking sheet.

Preheat the oven to 250°F. Line a rimmed baking sheet with a wire rack or paper towels. Place a high-walled skillet over medium-low heat, add the oil, and let it warm.

Working in batches, drop crab cakes into the bowl of panko and gently coat each cake with a light layer of the crumbs.

To check if the oil in the pan is hot enough, drop in a single bread crumb. If it begins to bubble and brown right away, the oil is ready for frying. Using a slotted spoon, carefully and gently lower each crab cake into the hot oil, being sure to place the cake away from you, towards the back of the stove in order to keep the oil from splattering. Cook, turning once, until the crab cakes are golden brown, about 2 minutes per side or until golden brown. Carefully transfer the browned crab cakes to the wire rack and keep warm in the oven. Repeat to coat and fry the remaining crab cakes.

Arrange the crab cakes on dollops of the reduced coconut milk mixture on serving plates and serve warm.

Mendocino Fish Stew

CLASSIC
BEAUJOLAIS

This stew is great for those looking for a simple way to cook fish fillets, like ling cod or petrale sole. Except for the fresh fish and basil, you may already have the rest of the ingredients in your refrigerator and pantry. And if you don't, consider stocking them for more flexibility and spontaneity in your meal prep. —MF

MAKES 4 SERVINGS

⅓ cup olive oil

2 cups minced yellow onions

2 tablespoons minced garlic

1 teaspoon Spanish smoked paprika

1¼ cups dry white wine

¾ cup canned fire-roasted crushed tomatoes

12 pimiento-stuffed green olives, cut in half

12 pitted kalamata olives, cut in half

2 tablespoons capers

1¾ teaspoons kosher salt

½ teaspoon freshly ground black pepper

Pinch of cayenne pepper

⅓ cup julienned fresh basil

Finely grated zest of 1 organic lemon

1½ pounds fresh ling cod or petrale sole fillets, cut into chunks about 2 inches square

Hot cooked pasta, boiled potatoes, or rice, for serving

½ cup minced fresh parsley, for garnish

Lemon wedges, for serving

In a 12-inch skillet over medium heat, warm the olive oil, then add the onions. Cook, stirring occasionally, until the onions have softened, 8 to 10 minutes. Stir in the garlic and cook until fragrant, 1 minute; do not let it brown. Stir in the smoked paprika, then add the wine. Increase the heat to medium-high and bring to a boil. Boil for 1 minute, then stir in the tomatoes, olives, capers, 1½ teaspoons of the salt, the pepper, and cayenne. Reduce the heat to medium and simmer for 1 minute. Sprinkle the basil over the surface of the tomato mixture, followed by the lemon zest. Working quickly, arrange the fish chunks on top of the tomato mixture, cover with a lid, and cook for 1 minute. Uncover the skillet, gently flip the fish, sprinkle with the remaining ¼ teaspoon salt, replace the lid, and cook until the fish is just flakable, 1 to 3 minutes, depending on the thickness of the fish.

To serve, divide the pasta, potatoes, or rice among wide, flat bowls and ladle the stew over the top. Sprinkle with parsley and place lemon wedges on the side for squeezing.

MODERN BEAUJOLAIS

Cioppino

MAKES 4 SERVINGS

SOUP BASE

½ cup extra-virgin olive oil

4 shallots, cut lengthwise into julienne

1 tablespoon fine sea salt

1 teaspoon freshly ground black pepper

12 garlic cloves, minced

1 tablespoon red pepper flakes or 1 Thai chile, chopped

1 cup low-alcohol dry red wine, such as Barbera, Pinot Noir, or Cabernet Franc

Two (32 ounce) cans whole peeled San Marzano tomatoes (I use di Napoli organic), crushed by hand to create a chunky mixture

2 cups Fish Stock (page 295) or water

12 whole basil leaves

1 bay leaf

CONTINUED

Cioppino, an Italian American tomato-based seafood stew, has developed a cult following around the San Francisco Bay Area and northern California. I've even overheard new diners at Cafe Beaujolais remark that they judge the chef's abilities by how good their cioppino is. It has become a staple on my menu during the cold and rainy winter months as a warming dish that shows off what the Pacific Ocean has to offer.

My Cioppino has three main components that are the foundations of the recipe, singing with high notes of briny and zingy flavors without masking the freshness of the fish. The first is a long-simmered onion-, garlic-, and tomato-infused soup base inspired by marinara sauce. This can be made the day of serving or a few days in advance. The second is a careful and meticulous layering of the fish and shellfish in the pan during the assembly of the stew. Each ingredient in cioppino requires its own unique cooking time in order to achieve the best flavor and texture. The last is a crisp, golden, and fragrant garlic toast to dip into the delicious juices. Sourdough bread, popular in the San Francisco Bay Area, is the classic choice.

To make the soup base, place a Dutch oven or heavy-bottomed pot over medium heat. When hot, add the oil, shallots, salt, and pepper. Cook, stirring, until the shallots become translucent, about 5 minutes. Add the garlic and red pepper or chile and cook, stirring, until fragrant, about 2 minutes. Add the wine and cook, stirring to scrape up any browned bits that may have accumulated on the bottom of the pot. Continue to cook until the wine has reduced to one-fourth of its volume and the mixture looks like a paste.

Add the crushed tomatoes, stock, basil, and bay leaf. Partially cover the pot, reduce the heat to low, and slowly simmer until the mixture has reduced by half, 45 to 60 minutes. You should end up with around 2 cups of soup base.

CONTINUED

Cioppino *(continued)*

- 2 tablespoons extra-virgin olive oil
- 2 cloves garlic, minced
- 2 dozen fresh littleneck clams in the shell, cleaned
- 2 dozen fresh large mussels in the shell, cleaned
- 1 cup dry white wine, such as Sauvignon Blanc, Pinot Grigio, or Dry Riesling
- 2 cups Fish Stock (page 295) or water
- 1 pound large shrimp (less than 15 per pound), peeled and deveined
- 1 pound fish fillets, such as rockfish, cod, salmon, or sablefish, cut into ½-inch chunks
- 6 to 12 diver scallops, cut into quarters
- 1 pound Dungeness crabmeat, other lump crabmeat, or lobster, picked over for shells and cartilage
- 1 tablespoon fine sea salt
- ½ cup room temperature unsalted butter
- Juice of 1 lemon
- Flat-leaf parsley leaves, for garnish

GARLIC TOASTS

- Extra-virgin olive oil, for drizzling
- Sliced sourdough bread, for serving
- 1 large garlic clove, halved

Remove the soup base from the heat and let cool to room temperature. If making the soup base ahead of time, transfer it to an airtight container and refrigerate for up to 1 week.

To cook the fish and shellfish, place a clean Dutch oven or large, heavy-bottomed pot with a lid on the stove and set over medium-high. Allow the pot to preheat for 1 to 2 minutes.

Working quickly, add the olive oil and garlic to the pan and sauté until golden brown, about 30 seconds. Quickly add the clams, mussels, and wine to the pot and cover with the lid. Cook the clams and mussels until all the shells have opened and they have released their juices into the pot, 4 to 5 minutes, depending on their size. With a slotted spoon or tongs, transfer each mussel and clam to a bowl, discarding any that failed to open.

Add 2 cups of the soup base and the seafood stock to the pot and bring to a boil. Meanwhile, remove the clam and mussel meat from the shells, discarding the shells. Set the shellfish meat aside.

When the soup base is boiling, add the shrimp, fish, and scallops to the pot and simmer until the seafood is around three-fourths cooked, 2 to 3 minutes. Turn off the heat and add the clam and mussel meat, crab meat, salt, butter, and lemon juice. Stir the ingredients thoroughly, cover the pot, and set aside to let the flavors meld.

To make the garlic toasts, preheat a cast-iron grill pan or sauté pan over medium-high heat. Drizzle olive oil over both sides of the sliced sourdough pieces and place them in the preheated pan. Cook each piece of bread until golden brown on each side, about 1 minute per side. Remove the toasted bread from the pan and rub one side with the garlic clove.

Divide the soup among large bowls and serve with the garlic toasts to soak up the juices.

Sound Adventure
613483

Basic Risotto

MAKES 4 SERVINGS

- 7 cups low-sodium vegetable broth, Chicken Stock (page 294), or water
- 2 tablespoons extra-virgin olive oil
- 1 medium yellow onion, minced
- 2 teaspoons fine sea salt
- 1 cup carnaroli or Arborio rice
- ½ cup dry white wine
- ½ cup butter
- ½ cup grated Parmigiano-Reggiano cheese

One of the beautiful facets of risotto is its versatility. Once you learn the basics of cooking risotto, it's easy to customize a dish to your own taste. Funnily, I learned how to first make risotto while I was staging at Le Moulin de Mougins, a Michelin-starred restaurant in Mougins, France. Don't tell my Italian friends, but I have stuck with the techniques I learned there ever since. Many people believe risotto to be a simple side dish or even an afterthought in a meal. The first bites of true risotto I had in France revealed to me that that was not true. With that one perfect bite, it occurred to me that Arborio or carnaroli rice—the basis of a true risotto—are the perfect vessel to transport whatever flavors you have on hand in the kitchen. I believe the texture of the risotto is the key. Every rice grain should have an "al dente" quality to it and each grain of rice should be distinguishable from the next. Basically this means that if the risotto is undercooked you will experience it as crunchy unappetizing rice grains, whereas if it is overcooked you will experience it as glutinous and sticky in texture. In either case, the flavors will not be what you remember. A perfect risotto will convey the flavors that you decide to add, and it will be a thing of beauty. The recipes that follow are a few of the many different variations I use at Cafe Beaujolais.

The hard part of this recipe is to know the exact timing of the recipe. Depending on the stove and the heat that is being used, the timing can be anywhere from 20 minutes to 35 minutes. It should be noted that the goal is to gradually allow the rice to absorb the stock. The true timing will not be known until the stock has been used and the rice is al dente, which is what makes the cooking of risotto such an intuitive technique.

Place the broth in a stock pot over high heat and bring to a boil. Once the broth is boiling, reduce the heat to low and let it simmer gently.

Place a Dutch oven or heavy-bottomed saucepan over medium-low heat. Add the olive oil and onion to the pot and sprinkle with the salt. Cook the onion, stirring occasionally with a wooden spoon. It is extremely important to not brown the onion, we are just aiming to sweat the water out. If the heat seems to be too high and you begin to see browning, reduce the heat and continue cooking. Once the onion has released the majority of its liquid and looks translucent, about 8 to 10 minutes later, stir in the rice. Continue to cook, stirring the rice so that each grain is coated by the oil. (This technique, which raises the temperature of the dry rice, is called "pearling" the rice. It is an important step to temper the rice grains, so that once liquid is added the rice soaks up the liquid at an even rate.) This should take about 2 minutes.

Add the wine and cook, scraping the bottom of the pan to release any bits that have stuck to the pan bottom. Cook until the wine has reduced and the fumes from the alcohol have dissipated, 2 to 3 minutes.

Using a ladle, slowly add 1 cup of broth to the rice. With a wooden spoon in hand, increase the heat to medium and stir the risotto gently but constantly. As the rice begins to cook, it will soften and will become brittle; gentle strokes with the wooden spoon are crucial. Allow the rice to absorb the first cup of broth, then add another cup of hot broth. Repeat this step as each cup of broth is absorbed.

After much of the broth has been absorbed, after about 20 to 35 minutes, taste the rice. If the rice grain is too firm, then you can continue cooking and add additional broth. If the rice is cooked, turn off the heat and gently fold in the butter and Parmigiano-Reggiano. You may not need all of the broth.

Serve immediately, scooped onto a large serving platter or into individual bowls or plates; this recipe is meant to be enjoyed as soon as the risotto has finished cooking.

Spring Pea Risotto

During late spring when English peas and pea tendrils are abundant, I like to highlight them on my menu in different ways, such as in this risotto. At Cafe Beaujolais we use this risotto as a starch base for many spring dishes such as lamb, salmon, and halibut. You can also enjoy it as a vegetarian main dish.

MAKES 4 SERVINGS

2 tablespoons extra-virgin olive oil

4 cloves garlic, minced

1 shallot, diced

1 cup freshly shucked English peas (frozen peas can be substituted)

½ cup crème fraîche

½ cup water

6 fresh mint leaves

6 fresh basil leaves

¼ cup unsalted butter, cubed

Finely grated zest and juice of 1 lemon

1 tablespoon fine sea salt

1 tablespoon freshly ground black pepper

Basic Risotto (page 164)

Pea tendrils, edible flowers, and finely grated lemon zest, for garnish

Warm a saucepan over medium heat. Add the olive oil, garlic, shallot, and a little pinch of salt and pepper and sauté until the shallots become translucent and garlic starts to become fragrant, 2 to 3 minutes. Add the peas, crème fraîche, and water. Bring the ingredients to a simmer and cook until the peas begin to soften, about 2 minutes. Immediately remove the pot from the heat and stir in the mint, basil, butter, lemon zest and juice, salt, and pepper.

Transfer the ingredients to a blender and blend on high speed until a puree forms. Set aside.

Cook the risotto as directed on page 164, but instead of adding the butter and Parmesan, fold in the pea puree. Divide the risotto among serving bowls and garnish with pea tendrils, edible flowers, and grated lemon zest. Serve warm.

Fall Butternut Squash Risotto

MAKES 4 SERVINGS

1 small butternut squash, about 1 pound, split lengthwise and seeds removed

2 tablespoons extra-virgin olive oil, plus more for drizzling

2 teaspoons fine sea salt

2 teaspoons freshly ground black pepper

8 garlic cloves

2 shallots, halved lengthwise

½ cup unsalted butter

Leaves from 1 small bunch fresh sage, plus small fresh sage leaves, for garnish

Juice of ½ lemon

Basic Risotto (page 164)

The key to this recipe is to allow the butternut squash to roast at a low, even temperature. This will allow the sugars in the squash to caramelize and release their sweetness. Risotto is one of my favorite starches thanks to its ability to carry the flavors of any vegetable or spice that it is showcasing. This recipe is a true representation of the fall season and all of the flavors that come with it. At Cafe Beaujolais, we feature this risotto on many different menu items. It works great with crispy duck confit and braised meat but also shines on its own as a main dish.

Preheat the oven to 350°F. Line a rimmed baking sheet with parchment paper.

Place the butternut squash halves skin-side down on the prepared baking sheet. Drizzle the squash with olive oil and season with 1 teaspoon each of the salt and pepper. Divide the garlic and shallots among the cavities of the squash. Roast until the squash is very soft and beginning to brown, about 1 hour. Remove the squash from the oven and let cool slightly.

Add the butter to a sauté pan over medium heat. Let the butter melt, then keep cooking it, maintaining heat, until it begins to brown slightly, 2 to 3 minutes. Remove the butter from the heat and carefully add the sage leaves and the lemon juice (the butter may splatter). Set aside.

Remove the skin from the cooked squash and place the flesh in a food processor. Add the remaining 1 teaspoon each salt and pepper and process until smooth. With the machine running, slowly add the sage-brown butter mixture until fully incorporated. Set aside.

Cook the risotto as directed on page 164, but instead of adding the butter and Parmesan, fold in the butternut squash mixture. Divide the risotto among serving bowls and garnish with a drizzle of olive oil and a few small fresh sage leaves. Serve warm.

Wild Mushroom Risotto

Wild mushrooms are an ingredient that we see at Cafe Beaujolais throughout the year. The first few years at Cafe Beaujolais I simply butter-sautéed them and placed them atop beautifully cooked Basic Risotto. It was a suitable way to showcase the mushrooms of Mendocino, but it lacked the full potential of a mushroom. I wrestled with different recipes and ideas of how to make the fungi "pop." The search for a heightened mushroom experience changed when a family friend named Francine Jack dined at the restaurant and walked me through a magical experience she had in Italy. Francine explained how she had a risotto that contained the stock of the mushroom along with a flavorful duxelles that was folded into the finished risotto. I tried these techniques in my recipe and never looked back. I hope you enjoy this technique—it's Francine-approved!

MAKES 4 SERVINGS

- 8 cups water
- 4 ounces dried porcini mushrooms
- 1 tablespoon grapeseed oil
- 1 pound assorted fresh wild mushrooms, such as porcini, chanterelle, and morel, roughly chopped
- 1 teaspoon fine sea salt
- 4 tablespoons unsalted butter
- 2 shallots, minced
- 2 cloves garlic, minced
- 4 sprigs fresh thyme
- ½ teaspoon freshly cracked black pepper
- Basic Risotto (page 164)

In a saucepan, bring the water to a boil over high heat. Once boiling, remove from the heat and add the dried porcini mushrooms. Let the mushrooms soak in the water for 15 minutes to rehydrate.

Scoop out the mushrooms, reserving the mushroom liquid to make the risotto. Roughly chop the rehydrated dried porcini and set aside.

Place a cast-iron skillet on the stove top over high heat. Add the oil, assorted wild mushrooms, including the rehydrated porcini mushrooms, and salt and sauté until the majority of the liquid has been released from the mushrooms, 5 to 10 minutes. Reduce the heat to medium low and add the butter, shallots, garlic, thyme sprigs, and pepper. Sauté until the shallots and garlic are softened, about 5 minutes. Transfer the mushroom mixture to a bowl and remove the thyme sprigs.

Cook the risotto as directed on page 164, using the porcini soaking water instead of stock. Fold the mushroom mixture into the finished risotto. Divide the risotto among serving bowls and serve warm.

Universal-Style Indian Curry

MAKES 6 SERVINGS

CURRY PASTE

½ cup crushed peeled ginger

10 cloves garlic

2 shallots, cut in half

2 dried bird's eye chiles

2 tablespoons turmeric powder

1 tablespoon cumin seeds, toasted

1 tablespoon coriander seeds, toasted

2 teaspoons fenugreek seeds

1 tablespoon fine sea salt

1 tablespoon freshly ground black pepper

Water, as needed

¼ cup coconut oil

1 tablespoon yellow mustard seeds

Two (13.5 ounce) cans unsweetened coconut milk

One (32 ounce) can whole Roma tomatoes, blended until smooth

6 curry leaves, each torn into two pieces

1 sweet potato, peeled and diced into ½-inch pieces

1 cup brown lentils

1 head cauliflower, cut into ¼-inch florets

1 bunch lacinato kale, stems removed and leaves cut into ribbons

Water, if needed

Fine sea salt

CONTINUED

The proper definition of a curry, according to the Oxford dictionary, is a South Asian dish of meat, vegetables, and aromatics cooked in a hot spicy sauce, often served with rice. But I tend to think of it simply as a dish that brings comfort and a healthy sensibility to one's diet and lifestyle. Regardless of the definition, curry is one of the most diverse, complex, yet simple recipe categories that you can make. I like to make this recipe whenever I have friends over to my house that I want to impress.

For me, the key to a delicious curry involves three main rules: First, make your curry paste from scratch. Next, be sure to cook the rawness out of the curry spices before proceeding with the recipe. Finally, serve your curry with flavorful, contrasting condiments, such as mango chutney and raita. The recipe that follows contains only vegetables and can easily be made vegan. In my mind it is the epitome of what a curry should be.

One of my favorite things about this recipe is that you must use your nose as a critical cooking tool! Be sure to smell the uncooked curry paste before adding it to the pot and reflect on the raw smell of the spices and vegetables. There is a sharpness to the smell that is hard to describe in writing, but you will understand when you sniff it. As the curry paste cooks and the water is released from the vegetables, the kitchen will be filled with a warm and soothing smell like no other.

To make the curry paste, in a blender, combine the ginger, garlic, shallots, chiles, turmeric, cumin, coriander, fenugreek, salt, and pepper and blend until a paste forms. Add a splash of water if needed to facilitate blending. If you're not using the curry paste right away, it can be frozen for up to 3 months.

CONTINUED

Universal-Style Indian Curry
(continued)

- Chopped fresh cilantro for garnish
- Southern Indian Coconut Rice (page 235) or warm naan bread, for serving (optional)
- Prepared mango chutney, for serving
- Raita (page 293), for serving

Warm a large Dutch oven over medium-high heat and add the coconut oil. When hot, add the mustard seeds—they should dance and pop in the hot oil—and cook for about 15 seconds. Add the curry paste and cook, stirring constantly, so that the paste does not burn. You will begin to smell the rawness dissipate of the shallot, garlic, and ginger and turn into a warm rich aroma, which should take 3 to 5 minutes.

When the curry paste is fragrant, add the coconut milk, blended tomatoes, curry leaves, sweet potatoes, and lentils. Bring the mixture to a simmer, reduce the heat to low, and cook, partially covered, until the sweet potatoes are tender, 30 to 40 minutes. Add the cauliflower and kale ribbons and continue to simmer until the cauliflower is tender, about 10 minutes. If the mixture seems too thick, add a ladle or two of water to loosen it. Taste the curry and adjust the seasoning with salt.

Divide the curry among bowls and sprinkle with cilantro. Serve warm with coconut rice or naan, if desired. Serve the chutney and raita on the side.

Pasta Bolognese

I have a special relationship with Bolognese. The dish is a staple in Northern Italian cuisine as well as in Hollywood mobster movies. It is the center of debate among many American Italian families: To use only one kind of meat? To add sugar or milk at the end of cooking? To use fresh tomatoes or canned? The debate is endless. Each professional chef I have worked for has developed his or her own interpretation of the dish. With an open mind, and drawing on my experience, I have created my own take on this Italian classic.

Like many Italian recipes, the ingredient list is short, but the understanding of the techniques is important and is what will differentiate a mediocre Bolognese from an outstanding one. Ingredients aside, the one constant with this recipe is that you cannot rush the sauce. Time is crucial in developing the deep and nuanced flavors of Bolognese. Using four basic techniques, anyone can create an incredible Bolognese.

First, we sweat the vegetables. All things that we consume contain some form of moisture and the majority of that moisture does not contribute to flavor. In order to achieve maximum flavor in this recipe we must try to extract and evaporate all possible moisture in the vegetables without browning them. Next, we render the fat. In short, rendering is the action of slowly cooking down fat into a liquid form. Cooking the meat low and slow ensures that the fat will melt and create a perfect medium in which to brown the meat. Then, we deglaze the liquid. The process of adding a liquid to a pan after sautéing ingredients lifts all of the sticky, browned bits on the bottom of the pot. These browned bits contribute a lot of flavor to a sauce. Finally, we reduce the sauce. After all of the ingredients have been added to the pot, we can further enhance the flavor of the sauce by slowly cooking it to bring down the volume. Reducing concentrates the flavors and helps them meld together into a singular, tasty sauce.

CONTINUED

MAKES 6 SERVINGS

- 2 large yellow onions, quartered
- 2 large carrots, peeled and chopped
- 6 stalks celery, chopped
- 4 cloves garlic
- 2 tablespoons fine sea salt
- 1 tablespoon freshly cracked black pepper
- ½ cup extra-virgin olive oil
- 1 pound ground beef
- 1 pound ground pork
- Two (6 ounce) cans tomato paste
- 2 bay leaves
- 1 bottle (750 ml) Sangiovese or Chianti Classico wine
- Leaves from 4 sprigs fresh thyme, chopped
- ½ cup unsalted butter, cut into cubes
- 1 pound pasta of your choice (I like tagliatelle or fettuccine)
- Freshly grated Parmigiano-Reggiano cheese, for serving

Pasta Bolognese *(continued)*

In a food processor, combine the onions, carrots, celery, garlic, salt, and pepper and pulse until a paste is formed.

Place a Dutch oven or large heavy-bottomed pot over medium-low heat and add the olive oil. When hot, add the vegetable paste and begin to sweat your vegetables. Cook, stirring often with a wooden spoon, so they don't brown, until very little visual steam comes from the pot, 15 to 30 minutes. If the heat seems too high and the vegetables are developing color, turn down the heat. Alternatively, if you do not see evaporating water coming from the pot, turn up the heat a bit.

Add the beef and pork to the pot and cook, using the spoon to break up the meat into uniformly small pieces, until the fat has melted and the meat is crispy and brown and has released all of its moisture, 60 to 90 minutes. Remember: our goal is to render the fat evenly and allow the protein to brown slowly. Stir the mixture every ten minutes or so to determine how much steam is leaving the pot.

Add the tomato paste and bay leaves and continue to cook, stirring occasionally, until the tomato paste begins to smell sweet, about 10 minutes.

Add the wine to the pan and reduce the heat to low. Cook, stirring up the browned bits on the bottom of the pan to deglaze it, and let the liquid simmer away. The sauce is ready when the wine has reduced by half its original volume, which usually takes about 1 hour. Remove from the heat and stir in the thyme and butter. Cover and keep warm.

Cook your favorite style of pasta in a large pot of boiling salted water until al dente. Using tongs, immediately transfer the cooked pasta straight from the water to the pot with the sauce, allowing a bit of the pasta water to fall in the sauce with the pasta. Stir to coat the pasta with the sauce. Divide the pasta among shallow bowls and set out the cheese for sprinkling.

Chicken with Mole Negro

MAKES 4 SERVINGS

MOLE NEGRO

- 1 large heirloom tomato, cut into chunks
- 3 tomatillos
- 1 sprig fresh thyme
- 12 cups Chicken Stock (page 294)
- 10 dried whole ancho pasilla chiles, seeds and stems removed and reserved
- 10 dried whole guajillo chiles, seeds and stems removed and reserved
- 5 dried whole chipotle meco chiles, seeds and stems removed and reserved
- 5 dried whole morita chiles, seeds and stems removed and reserved
- 1 yellow onion
- 1 head garlic, cloves peeled but kept whole
- 4 large tablespoons whole raw almonds
- 4 tablespoons shelled unsalted peanuts
- 4 whole raw pecans
- 1 cinnamon stick
- 6 whole black peppercorns
- 6 whole cloves
- 4 tablespoons grapeseed or peanut oil
- 3 tablespoons raisins
- 1 ripe plantain, peeled and sliced lengthwise
- 1 large slice brioche bread
- 1 cup sesame seeds
- 4 tablespoons lard
- 12 ounces bittersweet baking chocolate (80% or above), chopped

At Cafe Beaujolais we bring mole negro onto our menu once a year, usually in the late summer months when corn, tomatoes, and tomatillos are at their ripest and sweetest. It is a far stretch from any sort of French or Italian flavors, but it is a welcomed menu item by all diners at the cafe. This recipe takes a large amount of time and effort to make, but the results are well worth it. My advice: have your ingredients measured and prepped before embarking on this journey. My other tip: when cooking this recipe it is important to work in a well-ventilated area, whether that be opening all of the windows in your house and placing a fan in the area or working outside on a barbecue grill. The chiles will produce very intense fumes that will burn your lungs and eyes, so please prepare properly!

This mole can be served simply as a dipping sauce with tortilla chips or as the sauce to your fanciest whole roasted chicken. The idea is to think of the mole as a sauce that will provide a foundational flavor profile to whatever you may want to serve with it. During the late summer months that this sauce is on the Beaujolais menu I find myself making scrambled eggs in the morning and topping it with a tablespoon of mole.

Preheat the oven to 400°F.

Place the tomato, tomatillos, and thyme onto a baking sheet and place in the oven. Roast until the tomatoes and tomatillos begin to brown, about 20 minutes. Remove from the oven and let cool.

Pour the stock into a large pot and bring to a simmer. Place a large cast-iron skillet on the stovetop over high heat. Turn off the heat under the stock and set the pot next to the skillet.

Once the skillet is thoroughly preheated and smoking, working in batches, add the chiles to the dry pan and toast them in the hot skillet until each chile is thoroughly charred. This is a crucial step, as you want to char the chiles but not completely burn them. There is a fine line between charcoal colored, burned chile, and charred chiles—take care just to allow the outside skin of the chile to char and not the entire inside. This process should take 20 to 30 seconds per side for each chile. Once the chiles have charred, submerge them in the hot stock. This step will begin to soften the chiles and rehydrate them.

Next, add the chile seeds to the skillet and toast them until they are completely blackened, nearly burned. Don't be discouraged—this step will provide an amazing flavor to the mole. Add the blackened seeds to the stock. Cover the pot and let stand while you continue cooking the rest of the ingredients.

Turn the heat down to medium and add the onions and garlic to the dry skillet. Sauté the vegetables until well browned, 5 to 8 minutes. Remove from the pan and set aside. Add the almonds, peanuts, pecans, cinnamon stick, peppercorns, and cloves sauté until slightly toasted and fragrant, 1 to 2 minutes. Pour into a bowl and set aside.

Add 1 tablespoon of the oil to the skillet and then the raisins. Sauté for until the raisins rehydrate and double in size, about 1 minute. Transfer to the bowl with the nuts. Add another tablespoon of the oil to the skillet and sauté the plantains until they are golden brown on both sides, about 1 minute. Add the plantains to the bowl with the nuts and raisins.

Add another tablespoon of oil to the skillet, then add the brioche and toast until golden brown on both sides, about 30 seconds per side. Transfer to a plate.

CONTINUED

Citrus-Brined Chicken (page 200), carved into serving pieces

Mexican-Style Street Corn (page 243)

Chicken with Mole Negro
(continued)

Add the last tablespoon oil to the skillet and toast the sesame seeds until browned, up to 5 minutes depending on how hot the pan is. Transfer the sesame seeds to a high-speed blender. Add 1 cup of the stock and blend until a paste forms, you may need to add more stock if the mixture isn't becoming smooth. Transfer the paste to a large bowl. Pour the remaining stock along with the soaking chiles and seeds in the same blender and blend until smooth. This mixture will be called our chile paste. Transfer the chile paste to a small bowl.

Using the same blender, begin adding the rest of the ingredients in batches: the onions, garlic, tomatoes, tomatillos, brioche, nuts, and spices. Blend the ingredients until smooth and transfer to another bowl.

Heat a large Dutch oven or stock pot over medium heat. Add the lard and the chile paste and cook until some of the extra liquid cooks off, 5 to 10 minutes. Add the remainder of the blended ingredients and reduce the heat so the mixture just simmers. Let the mixture simmer to blend the flavors, stirring every 3 to 5 minutes, for 30 minutes, being careful not to let the mixture scorch the bottom. Turn the heat off and stir in the chocolate until melted.

To serve, divide the mole among serving plates, creating a pool in the bottom of each plate. Arrange the chicken and corn on each plate and serve right away.

To save the mole for another meal, let it cool and then store in an airtight container for up to 10 days in the refrigerator or up to 3 months in the freezer.

Black Cod with Agnolotti, Beets, Bok Choy, and Truffle-Madeira Sauce

When I first arrived as chef at Cafe Beaujolais I inherited a dinner menu that had not been radically changed for decades. Dishes were still being served that were revolutionary to the diners of the 1980s and 90s but lacking the inspiration that many of the 21st-century "foodies" have come to expect at their favorite restaurants. I began to innovate and update the dinner menu at the cafe slowly in order to allow time for the longtime patrons of Cafe Beaujolais to adjust to a novel dining experience. There was one dish in particular that was beloved by the clientele that frequented the cafe—the sturgeon. The most advice I received by longtime diners was to not take the sturgeon off the dinner menu. Sturgeon is not a native fish of the Mendocino Coast, and deep down my goal was to create a more local-centric menu. I had to be careful and meticulous in developing a suitable replacement that would excite new diners yet still allow long-time guests an experience that would rival that favorite dish. After being at the cafe for two years, I decided to take the leap and put this black cod dish on the menu. It ended up being the perfect replacement.

MAKES 4 SERVINGS

MADEIRA SAUCE

6 cups unsalted Chicken Stock (page 294)

1 ounce dried morels

2 salt-packed anchovy fillets, de-boned, rinsed, and soaked in milk for 15 minutes

1 tablespoon capers

1 large garlic clove, minced

½ cup Madeira

MUSHROOM DUXELLES

3 tablespoons grapeseed oil

Reconstituted morel mushrooms from the Madeira Sauce (above), chopped

8 ounces shiitake mushrooms, stems removed and sliced

8 ounces cremini mushrooms, sliced

2 cloves garlic, minced

2 shallots, diced

Leaves from 1 sprig fresh thyme

4 tablespoons crème fraîche

4 tablespoons unsalted butter

4 tablespoons mascarpone cheese

PASTA DOUGH

1¾ cups 00 flour, or more as needed

6 egg yolks

1 whole egg

1 tablespoon milk

1 teaspoon extra-virgin olive oil

CONTINUED

To make the Madeira Sauce, in a saucepan over medium-high heat, combine the stock and dried morels. When the liquid simmers, reduce the heat to low and simmer until the mushrooms have rehydrated, 15 minutes. Strain the stock into a clean saucepan and reserve the mushrooms. Place the stock over high heat and bring to a boil. Cook until the stock has reduced to 1 cup, about 20 minutes; the liquid will be concentrated and flavorful.

CONTINUED

Black Cod with Agnolotti, Beets, Bok Choy, and Truffle-Madeira Sauce *(continued)*

- Roasted Baby Beets (page 246; omit the pecorino and mint)
- 2 heads bok choy
- 1 cup semolina
- Fine sea salt
- Extra-virgin olive oil
- 4 tablespoons unsalted butter
- Four 6-ounce black cod fillets, skin removed, patted dry
- 2 tablespoons grapeseed oil
- 2 tablespoons truffle butter

Drain the anchovies, discarding the milk, and then coarsely chop them. Add the chopped anchovies to a small saucepan along with the capers, garlic, and Madeira. Turn the heat to medium-high and carefully bring the mixture to a boil until the alcohol smell dissipates, 2 to 3 minutes. (Take care, as there is a chance that the alcohol will ignite. Don't worry; this is a natural process. Keep your head away from the flames—they will dissipate in several seconds.) Add the reduced stock to the pan and bring back to a boil. Once boiling, remove from the heat and let cool. Store the cooled mixture in the refrigerator until ready to serve. (This mixture can be made in advance and stored in the refrigerator in an airtight container for up to 10 days).

To make the Mushroom Duxelles, place a large sauté pan over high heat. Add the grapeseed oil, reconstituted morels, shiitakes, and creminis and sauté until the majority of the liquid has been released from the mushrooms, 8 to 10 minutes. Add the garlic, shallots, and thyme and cook until the shallots turn translucent, about 5 minutes. Turn off the heat and stir in the crème fraîche, butter, and mascarpone. Place the mushroom mixture in a blender and blend on high speed until smooth. Transfer the mixture to an airtight container and place in the refrigerator until ready to assemble. (This mixture can be made in advance and stored in the refrigerator in an airtight container for up to 10 days.)

To make the Pasta Dough, pour the 00 flour into a pile on a flat kitchen work surface and create a well in the center. Add the egg yolks, egg, milk, and olive oil into the flour well. Using a fork, begin to whisk the egg mixture, slowly bringing in small amounts of flour into the mixture, until the mixture starts to thicken and resemble dough. At this point, set the fork aside and use your hands to knead the dough until it comes together and is smooth to the touch, about 10 minutes. Wrap the dough with plastic wrap and refrigerate for about 30 minutes.

While the pasta is chilling, follow the instructions on page 246 to prepare the Roasted Baby Beets.

Next, bring a pot of water to a boil over high heat. Have ready a bowl of ice water next to the stove. Cut the root off each bok choy so that the leaves are separated. Place the bok choy into the boiling water and cook for 2 minutes. Using a slotted spoon or kitchen tongs, transfer the bok choy into the ice bath and let sit in the ice water for about 5 minutes. Drain and pat the leaves dry with a kitchen towel. Set aside.

To shape the Agnolotti, remove the pasta dough from the refrigerator and unwrap it. Cut the dough into 4 equal pieces. Following the manufacturer's instructions, roll each dough piece through a standard pasta machine into long, thin sheets to the number 1 setting—thin enough that you can see your fingers through the pasta sheet. As you work, place the sheets on a work surface. Using a sharp knife, cut the pasta sheets so that they are 3 inches wide and 2 feet long. Transfer the mushroom mixture to a piping bag.

Starting from your left and working to your right, pipe a continuous ½-inch-wide strip of the mushroom mixture across the center of the pasta sheet. Fold the side closest to your body to the opposite side, like you're folding a blanket. Using your index finger, press down firmly at 1-inch intervals to make 1-inch pillow-shapes, then use a knife to separate each section into individual pieces. Cut the pasta where the presses were created. Line a baking sheet with a thin layer of semolina, place the finished agnolotti onto the baking sheet, and set aside until you're ready to cook.

Now that your prep is finished, you can begin to assemble the final dish. Remove the Madeira Sauce from the refrigerator. Preheat the oven to 400°F. Bring about 8 cups of water and ¼ cup sea salt to a boil in a large pot over high heat. Once boiling turn the heat down to medium and simmer. Place the bok choy leaves on a baking sheet, drizzle with about ¼ cup olive oil, and sprinkle with 1 teaspoon of salt. Roast until the bok choy begins to brown slightly, about 15 minutes.

CONTINUED

Black Cod with Agnolotti, Beets, Bok Choy, and Truffle-Madeira Sauce *(continued)*

Place a 10- to 12-inch sauté pan over medium-low heat, add the chopped beets and about ½ cup of the pasta water. Place the agnolotti into the big pot of simmering water and cook until the agnolotti float to the surface of the water, 3 to 4 minutes. Using a strainer, remove the agnolotti from the pot and transfer them to the pan containing the beets. Add 2 tablespoons of the unsalted butter and cook until the butter melts and the pasta turns a purple color, roughly 2 minutes. Set the pasta and beets aside and keep warm.

Season both sides of the black cod fillets with 1 teaspoon sea salt. Place a cast-iron skillet or heavy-bottomed ovenproof sauté pan over high heat. Once the pan begins to smoke, add the grapeseed oil and carefully place the black cod fillets into the pan, skin side up. You will hear a loud searing sound. Immediately place the pan with the fish into the oven. Cook until the fish firms up and slightly flakes when pressed, 7 to 10 minutes.

Using oven mitts, remove the pan from the oven and put the pan on a burner over medium-high heat. Add ½ cup of the Madeira Sauce (save the rest for another use), the truffle butter, and the remaining 2 tablespoons of unsalted butter to the pan. Carefully flip the fish using a spatula. Cook for 1 minute or until the butter has melted.

To assemble the dish, place 4 agnolotti along with 5 to 6 beet pieces, onto each warm serving plate. Roll the cooked bok choy leaves around your index fingers, then place 5 onto each plate surrounding the pasta. Place a cooked cod fillet atop the agnolotti and drizzle the truffle butter sauce from the pan over each portion of fish. Enjoy!

A Brief History of Café Beaujolais

- Starters -
Fall Kale Salad
Local Heirloom Caprese
Chopped Mixed Green Salad
Ahi Tartare Crostini
Seared Hudson Valley Foie Gras
Suggested Wine Pairing
Charred Spanish Octopus
Vietnamese Prawn Salad
Liberty Farms Duck Confit
- Pasta -
- Main -
- Sides -

Chinese Five-Spiced Duck Breast

MAKES 4 SERVINGS

6 whole star anise pods

1½ teaspoon whole cloves

1 whole cinnamon stick

2 tablespoons fennel seeds

2 teaspoons Szechuan peppercorns

4 teaspoons fine sea salt

1 teaspoon grapeseed oil

4 duck breast halves

SEASONAL FRUIT GASTRIQUE (OPTIONAL)

1 cup granulated sugar

1 cup red wine vinegar

2 cups Beef Stock (page 294)

½ teaspoon fine sea salt

1 cup sliced fresh cherries, figs, quince, kumquats, or other seasonal fruit

Over the years of cooking in the kitchen I have been asked the question, "What is your signature dish?" or "What is your favorite dish to cook?" I have never had a concrete answer but usually said, "Whatever I am cooking next is my favorite," emphasizing my love for cooking and the desire to do nothing else as a profession. One afternoon as I was developing a new spring menu I began to reflect on my menu over the past eight years. I realized that the duck breast in its many various iterations has never left my menu. Is this my signature dish? I did not concede to the idea completely, but if there was any dish that was close enough to a signature, this would be it.

At Cafe Beaujolais, the seasons dictate what fruit I pair with the duck breast on the menu. In the spring, I pair the meat with cherries harvested from local trees. In the summer, I use figs. In the fall, I use quince. In the winter, I favor kumquat. Seasonal fruit paired with duck is one of the best matches in the world of food pairings. I urge you as a home cook to experiment with various fresh and dried fruits to find what you enjoy the most.

After finding a suitable fruit accompaniment, the next key to a delicious duck breast is to ensure a crispy skin while maintaining a medium-rare to medium internal temperature to the meat. The key to crispy duck skin is to remove as much water content as possible. In my restaurant kitchen we buy the ducks whole and air-dry them in our walk-in refrigerator for a minimum of 2 weeks. This type of intense drying is not practical for the home cook, so I have created a workaround with great results. Here is a step-by-step guide to help you do it at home.

In a sauté pan over medium heat, toast the star anise, cloves, cinnamon stick, fennel seed, and Szechuan peppercorns until golden and fragrant, 2 to 3 minutes. Remove from the heat. Transfer the spices to a spice grinder and blend until smooth.

Season the duck breasts with a teaspoon of the spice blend along with 1 teaspoon of sea salt per breast. Rub the salt and spices onto both sides of the duck breast.

Place the duck breast fat side up on a plate lined with a paper towel. Place the plate in the refrigerator, unwrapped, and allow to air dry in the refrigerator for up to 3 days.

Score the duck skin in a diagonal, ¼-inch crosshatch pattern. A precise scoring of the duck breast's skin allows the fat to properly render. The key is to just cut through the skin and avoid cutting down to the actual duck meat. You'll want to use an extremely sharp knife, or you can go to your local hardware store and purchase a disposable razor blade for this task.

Coat the cold pan with the oil (this helps get the fat rendering process started). Lay the duck breast skin-side down in the pan and turn the burner to medium-low heat. Let the duck cook until the majority of the fat has been rendered, 4 to 5 minutes. Keep the fat in the pan and turn the duck over and allow to cook in its own fat. I like to achieve this by placing the duck in the corner of the pan and tilting the pan slightly so the fat can cover more of the breast. If you desire a medium-rare duck breast this step will take around 2 minutes.

Transfer the duck breasts to a plate or metal rack and allow them to rest before slicing. This process allows the duck to finish cooking naturally without overcooking, as the temperature will continue to rise after removing the duck breast from the pan. It also lets the internal juices to settle so that they will not run out while slicing.

If making the Seasonal Fruit Gastrique, place a heavy saucepan over medium-high heat. Add the sugar and cook, without stirring. In 3 to 5 minutes, the sugar will melt and begin to change color. Once it turns an amber brown color, remove it from the heat. Slowly add the vinegar to the saucepan, while gently making a clockwise motion with the saucepan to stir the mixture. It is important to not use a utensil during this stage so that the sugar will not crystallize. Once the vinegar has been incorporated, place the pan back over medium-high heat and cook until the liquid is reduced to about ¼ cup, about 5 minutes.

Add the stock and continue to cook over high heat until the liquid has reduced and a saucelike consistency has been achieved, 8 to 10 minutes. Season with salt and stir in the seasonal fruit.

Using a sharp knife, thinly slice the duck breasts across the grain. This step is very important as the duck breast will be much more tender in thin slices. Enjoy these duck breasts on their own or with the Seasonal Fruit Gastrique and your favorite sides.

Duck Confit

MAKES 6 SERVINGS

6 duck legs, about 3 pounds

6 tablespoons fine sea salt

3 tablespoons sugar

3 cloves garlic

1 bunch fresh flat-leaf parsley, stems and leaves

Leaves from 6 sprigs thyme

1 tablespoon freshly ground black pepper

3 bay leaves

Finely grated zest of 1 orange

4 cups rendered duck fat

Duck confit is a well-loved classic French dish. We at Cafe Beaujolais take pride in serving it in many various dishes throughout the restaurant. Duck fat is the primary ingredient in this recipe and it has luckily become much more readily available in the marketplace. Most specialty grocers carry tubs of it on their shelves. Don't be alarmed at the quantity of fat it takes to make this recipe. Give it a chance and hopefully duck confit will become a fixture on your home menus just like it has become a fixture at Cafe Beaujolais. A wonderful reason to make this is the leftover duck fat it creates. Let the remaining duck fat in the Dutch oven cool to room temperature. Transfer the cooled duck fat to an airtight container and place it in the freezer for up to 6 months. You can reuse the fat for sautéing potatoes or when you want to make duck confit again.

Rinse the duck legs under cold water and set aside to drain. In a food processor, combine the salt, sugar, garlic, parsley, thyme, pepper, bay leaves, and orange zest and blend until the texture is like that of wet sand. Transfer the salt-herb mixture to a 1-gallon-size locking plastic bag and add the duck legs. Massage the salt-herb mixture into the duck legs, coating them thoroughly. Place the sealed bag in the refrigerator and let the duck legs marinate for 24 hours.

Preheat the oven to 325°F. Rinse the salt-herb mixture from the duck legs and dry with paper towels. Be sure that all of the mixture is removed. In a saucepan over low heat, melt the duck fat and pour into a Dutch oven. Place the rinsed and dried duck legs into the fat, being sure that each leg is fully submerged. Place in the oven and cook gently until the duck legs are tender to the touch but not falling off the bone, 2½ to 3 hours. Remove the duck legs from the oven and let cool to room temperature.

When cool, cover the duck legs, still submerged in the fat, and place in the refrigerator until ready to serve. The duck fat acts to preserve the duck meat, so you can store them in the refrigerator for up to 3 months, tightly covered and submerged in the fat.

To serve, preheat the oven to 400°F. Line a baking sheet with a metal rack or line a platter with paper towels. Warm a nonstick, ovenproof skillet over medium-high heat. Add 1 tablespoon of rendered duck fat (removed from the fat used to cook the duck legs) to the skillet and heat. After about 1 to 2 minutes, you'll notice that the fat has developed a sheen. At that point, add the duck legs to the pan skin-side down and place the skillet in the oven. Roast until the skin has turned a deep, dark brown, about 10 minutes. Transfer the duck legs to the rack or platter and allow the fat to drain. Serve warm.

Chicken Stuffed Under the Skin

CLASSIC BEAUJOLAIS

The original recipe for this dish used a whole chicken and a technique called spatchcocking. While not a term you run across every day, it's one to learn since it could easily transform the way you prepare whole chickens—and turkeys, for that matter. The word refers to removing the bird's backbone (sharp poultry shears are a must), flipping it over so the breast side is up, then pressing firmly on the breastbone to crack it, which flattens the bird. With spatchcocking, the roasting time is shorter and the skin gets evenly browned, a double-plus. After that grand introduction, I'll say that when I haven't wanted or needed to prepare an entire bird, I've used thighs instead, which is faster and less fussy, much more suited to my life these days. —MF

MAKES 6 TO 8 SERVINGS

- 12 ounces natural cream cheese or soft goat cheese
- 1 egg
- 1 egg yolk
- 3 ounces Parmigiano-Reggiano cheese, finely grated
- 1 to 2 medium zucchini
- 1 cup finely chopped yellow onion
- ¼ cup olive oil
- 4 cloves garlic, minced
- 3 tablespoons fresh basil ribbons
- 1 tablespoon minced fresh thyme leaves
- 2 teaspoons minced fresh tarragon
- 2 teaspoons minced fresh rosemary
- 4 teaspoons kosher salt
- ½ teaspoon freshly ground black pepper
- Finely grated zest from 1 organic lemon
- 1 whole chicken, 3 to 4 pounds, or 8 to 10 bone-in, skin-on chicken thighs

In the bowl of an electric mixer or by hand, blend the cream cheese or goat cheese, whole egg and yolk, and Parmesan. Set aside.

Using the large holes on a box grater, coarsely grate the zucchini (do not use the fine holes, or the vegetable will disappear into the stuffing mixture). You need 1½ cups grated zucchini; reserve the rest for another use.

In a large pan over medium heat, sauté the onion in the olive oil until soft and translucent, 5 to 10 minutes. Increase the heat to medium-high, then add the grated zucchini, garlic, basil, thyme, tarragon, rosemary, 1½ teaspoons of the salt, and the pepper. Stir or toss to combine, and sauté and stir until just tender, about 5 minutes. The goal is to get the vegetables dry to prevent the filling from being too wet.

Scrape the vegetable mixture into a strainer and let the liquid drip out. Let strain and cool for 20 minutes, pressing lightly a couple of times. (Any collected liquid makes a delicious addition to scrambled eggs or just mop it up with bread.)

CONTINUED

Chicken Stuffed Under the Skin *(continued)*

In a bowl, mix together the vegetable and cheese mixtures and the lemon zest, and blend thoroughly. Refrigerate for up to 1 hour.

Preheat the oven to 375°F.

To stuff a whole chicken: Remove the giblets and liver, and any extra fat. Starting at the tail end, use poultry shears to cut out the backbone and save for stock. Turn the chicken skin side up with the wings closest to you. Flatten the chicken by pressing firmly on the breastbone until you hear it crack. Flip the chicken back over and sprinkle the remaining 2½ teaspoons salt over the surface, and then flip back again so the breast side is facing up.

Loosen the skin carefully by slipping your hand between the skin and flesh, moving your hand gently around the breast and into the thigh. You will make it a couple of inches down the drumstick.

You can stuff the chicken with your hand, but I always find it easier and less messy with a pastry bag. If you don't have a pastry bag, use a 1-gallon-size locking plastic bag. Snip off one bottom corner with a diagonal cut and insert a large pastry tip to wedge it in the cut corner. It should fit snugly. Fill the bag no more than half full with the vegetable-cheese mixture.

To insert the stuffing, put the point of the pastry tip under the chicken skin where you have loosened it, and move (don't squeeze the bag yet!) down to the thigh. Then, squeeze slowly and gently to press the filling as far down into the drumstick as it can easily go. Work your way up into the thigh, gently smoothing out the stuffing with your other hand. Finish with the breast. You may have some stuffing leftover, depending on the size of the bird.

Place the stuffed bird on a large, rimmed baking sheet and roast until the skin is richly browned and an instant-read thermometer registers 165°F when inserted into the flesh, away from the bone, about 1 hour. If the skin starts to brown too quickly, loosely cover with a piece of foil about 15 minutes before the end of roasting. Remove the bird from the oven, cover lightly with foil, and let stand for 5 to 10 minutes before cutting into serving pieces. Serve hot.

To stuff chicken thighs, sprinkle 1½ teaspoons of the salt on the underside of the thighs and turn them skin-side up. Using your fingers, carefully loosen the skin around the part of the thigh where it comes off most easily; you may need a paring knife to help—you're creating a pocket for the stuffing.

Using a teaspoon, spoon some of the stuffing into the pocket, then gently press the stuffing as far down under the skin of the thigh as you can. Add more stuffing and repeat until you've used approximately the correct amount of stuffing for the number of thighs you are planning to stuff. With your hand, work to gently smooth out the filling under the skin so it sits in a smooth layer. Repeat with the remaining thighs and filling.

Place the stuffed thighs skin side up in a baking dish large enough to hold them in a single layer. Sprinkle with the remaining 1 teaspoon salt. Roast until the skin is beautifully browned and an instant-read thermometer registers 165°F when inserted into the flesh, away from the bone, 30 to 35 minutes. Serve hot.

MODERN BEAUJOLAIS

Citrus-Brined Chicken

MAKES 4 TO 6 SERVINGS

CITRUS BRINE

4 quarts water

¼ cup honey

¾ cup fine sea salt

1½ tablespoons red pepper flakes

3 lemons, halved

1 lime, halved

1 whole chicken, 3 to 4 pounds

SAUCE

2 pounds chicken bones

½ pound chicken feet

Grapeseed oil

½ pound cremini mushrooms, quartered

2 shallots, diced

2 cloves garlic, smashed

½ teaspoon fine sea salt

2 tablespoons tomato paste

1 cup dry white wine

1 cup Beef Stock (page 294)

1 cup Chicken Stock (page 294)

½ bunch fresh parsley

4 sprigs fresh thyme

8 whole peppercorns

1 bay leaf

2 tablespoons unsalted butter

1 garlic clove

1 sprig of thyme

2 tablespoons unsalted butter

In my opinion, chicken is the most underrated main dish on fine-dining menus. While working at the restaurant Mar'Sel under Chef Charles Olalia I learned how to prepare and serve amazingly flavorful chicken that stood up to the more popular steaks and seafood. This recipe is inspired from my time there. In order to unlock the full flavor potential of the bird, I like to brine it before cooking. Then, in order to get the sought after crispy skin, I air-dry my chickens in the refrigerator.

The sauce for this chicken is based on the classic French Sauce Poulet and is a touch complicated, but I promise it is worth the extra effort. The addition of chicken feet in the sauce adds depth and richness—trust me on this! The combination of both beef and chicken stocks creates a delicious and balanced finished product. The good news? The sauce freezes well and can be made in advance—it will last up to 3 months in your freezer. It's a great project on a rainy weekend. Serve this dish over mashed potatoes or with roasted vegetables.

To make the Citrus Brine, in a pot, combine the water, honey, salt, and red pepper flakes. Set over high heat and bring to a simmer, stirring to dissolve the salt and honey. Remove from the heat and juice the citrus halves into the water. Toss the juiced lemons and lime into the water as well. Let the brine cool to room temperature.

Remove the giblets and liver, and any extra fat from the chicken. Starting at the tail end, use poultry shears to cut out the backbone and save for stock. Turn the chicken skin side up with the wings closest to you. Removing the wing tip and the middle bone from the wing, so that there is only one bone left on the wing. Flatten the chicken by pressing firmly on the breastbone until you hear it crack.

CONTINUED

Citrus-Brined Chicken
(continued)

Flip the chicken back over and, using a boning knife, debone the leg and thigh bones to create a boneless leg and thigh that is still connected to the main body of the chicken. Reserve the removed bones for the sauce.

Transfer the brine to a stock pot that will fit the entire bird with the brine and add the prepared chicken. Refrigerate the chicken in the brine for a minimum for 3 hours and up to 5 hours.

Remove the chicken from the brine and pat dry with paper towels. For best results, place the chicken on a rimmed baking sheet and refrigerate, uncovered for at least 1 hour or overnight, if possible, to allow the skin to dry out completely.

To make the Sauce, set a large Dutch oven over medium-high heat. When hot, add 2 tablespoons grapeseed oil and carefully add the chicken bones. Let the bones sear without disturbing them in order to ensure a nice brown crust. After about 5 minutes, turn the bones to brown on the other side. Transfer the bones to a paper towel lined baking sheet.

Reduce the heat to medium and add the mushrooms, shallots, garlic, and salt. Sauté until the vegetables have softened, about 5 minutes. Add the tomato paste and sauté for 2 minutes. Add the wine and cook, stirring, until the pan begins to dry and the wine has been completely reduced, about 10 minutes. Add the browned chicken bones, the chicken feet, both stocks, parsley, thyme, peppercorns, and bay leaf. Bring the liquid to a simmer and let cook until the liquid has reduced to a sauce-like consistency, 30 to 60 minutes.

Carefully strain the sauce through a fine-mesh strainer into a clean pot; discard the solids. Stir the butter into the sauce until melted and set it aside.

Preheat the oven to 450°F. Place a large cast-iron skillet over high heat. Add a small amount of grapeseed oil to the pan and place the chicken skin side down. Immediately place the pan into the oven. Roast until the chicken is semi-firm to the touch and an instant-read thermometer registers 165°F when inserted into the flesh, about 15 minutes.

Protecting your hand with an oven mitt, transfer the pan to a burner over medium heat. Add 2 tablespoons butter, 1 smashed garlic clove, and a sprig of thyme. Baste the chicken with the flavored butter and transfer to a carving board to rest for 10 minutes.

Reheat the sauce. Carve the chicken into serving pieces and ladle the sauce over the top.

Halibut in Parchment with Fingerling Potatoes, Tomatoes, Olives, and Herbs

Steaming fish in parchment paper allows the fish to stay moist and not overcook while simultaneously imparting all of the flavors of the other ingredients you decide to add to the paper vessel. I have used this recipe numerous times for dinner parties and small gatherings. It requires a small amount of prep and limits clean up responsibilities as you can just dump the used parchment paper into the bin once you are finished. This recipe follows a classic Southern Italian flavor profile, but feel free to add whatever aromatics and herbs you like. Halibut is used here but any fish can be used as a substitute.

MAKES 4 SERVINGS

- 1 pound fingerling potatoes
- 4 halibut fillets, 6 to 8 ounces each
- ⅔ cup high-quality Castelvetrano olives, pitted and quartered
- ½ cup capers
- 1 red onion, thinly sliced
- 1 clove garlic, minced
- 1 cup cherry tomatoes, sliced lengthwise
- 3 lemons, thinly sliced
- 1 bunch fresh thyme
- 1 bunch fresh oregano
- ½ cup dry white wine
- ½ cup high-quality extra-virgin olive oil
- 2 teaspoons fine sea salt
- 1 teaspoon freshly cracked black pepper

Place the fingerling potatoes into a saucepan with cold water to cover. Place over high heat and bring the water to a boil. Reduce the heat to medium-low and simmer until the potatoes are tender, 15 to 20 minutes. Drain the potatoes and transfer them to a baking sheet to cool.

While the potatoes are cooling, preheat the oven to 375°F. Cut a sheet of parchment paper about 24 inches square. Place the parchment on a low-rimmed baking sheet.

Using the palm of your hand, gently smash the cooled potatoes into a layer in the center of the parchment paper. Top with the halibut fillets.

In a bowl, combine the olives, capers, onion, garlic, tomatoes, lemon slices, thyme, oregano, white wine, olive oil, salt, and pepper, and mix well. Spoon the mixture over the fish. Lifting the two opposite sides of the parchment to meet in the middle above the fish. Crimp the ends to seal and create a rough boat shape to enclose the ingredients completely. You are trying to trap the steam inside the packet as the fish cooks. If needed, you can use toothpicks to seal the parchment.

Bake the parchment packet until the halibut begins to flake and is evenly white and not translucent, 15 to 25 minutes depending on the thickness of the halibut fillets.

To serve, carefully transfer the packet to a serving platter and present at the table. Use a large spoon to spoon the ingredients onto serving plates.

Moroccan Lamb Shanks

MAKES 4 SERVINGS

- 1 tablespoon fine sea salt, plus more to taste
- 2 tablespoons high-smoke-point oil, such as grapeseed oil
- 4 lamb foreshanks
- ¼ cup ras el hanout
- 1 tablespoon sweet paprika
- 1 tablespoon ground turmeric
- 1 teaspoon ground cumin
- 1 teaspoon cayenne pepper
- ¼ cup tomato paste
- 4 cups Chicken Stock or Beef Stock (page 294), or water
- 4 carrots, peeled and cut into ½-inch pieces
- 4 celery stalks, cut into 1-inch pieces
- 2 yellow onions, cut into large dice
- 6 garlic cloves, crushed
- 1-inch knob ginger, peeled and crushed
- 1 cinnamon stick
- 4 bay leaves
- 1 orange, washed and cut in half
- ½ cup unsalted butter, at room temperature

GARNISH

- ½ cup plain yogurt
- ½ cup sesame seeds, toasted (see page 295)
- ½ cup peanuts, chopped and toasted (see page 295)
- Leaves from 1 bunch fresh cilantro
- Leaves from 1 bunch fresh mint, chopped
- Juice of 1 lemon

Lamb shanks should not be looked at with fear. They can be found at most butcher counters. Through slow cooking and proper techniques, they can be turned into one of the most flavorful cuts. This recipe is based on the classic tagine of Morocco where there is no shortage of flavors to excite the palate. The key spice in this recipe is ras el hanout, which in Arabic means "top of the shop." In the markets of Arab countries, spice shops will combine their top spices with the intention of making their own house spice blend. Each ras el hanout will be different tasting but through my experience the blend will always create an exquisitely flavored dish. Serve with couscous, your favorite rice, mashed potatoes, or creamy polenta.

Preheat the oven to 325°F.

Place a large Dutch oven or heavy-bottomed, ovenproof pot on the stovetop over medium-high heat. When hot, sprinkle the salt evenly into the pot and add the oil. Carefully place the lamb shanks into the pot (if the pot can only fit 2 lamb shanks, you can work in 2 batches). You should hear an aggressive sizzle. Cook, turning as needed, until the lamb shanks have an even golden-brown color, 2 to 3 minutes per side. Carefully transfer the browned lamb shanks to a baking sheet or plate lined with paper towels.

Turn down the heat to medium-low and let the heat level off for a minute or two. Add the ras el hanout, paprika, turmeric, cumin, and cayenne to the fat in the pan and immediately stir with a wooden spoon, which will form a paste. Continue to cook, stirring and scraping the paste and the browned bits (or fond) until the raw spices lose their intensity and take on a "warm," soothing aroma, 30 to 60 seconds. Add the tomato paste and stir aggressively until a thicker paste forms, another 30 to 60 seconds. Add the stock, increase the heat to high, and bring the liquid to a boil.

CONTINUED

Moroccan Lamb Shanks
(continued)

Using a wooden spoon, stir and scrape the browned bits from the bottom of the pan.

Add the carrots, celery, onions, garlic, ginger, cinnamon stick, bay leaves, and orange to the boiling liquid. When the mixture returns to a boil, immediately cover the pot with the lid and place in the preheated oven. Cook in the oven until the lamb shanks are fork tender, but are not yet falling off the bone, 2 to 3 hours. It is important to begin to check the meat at the 2-hour mark. To do this, gently press on the lamb shanks with kitchen tongs or a large spoon. The meat is cooked when it begins to fall apart and separate from the bone.

Remove the pot from the oven and lower the oven temperature to 225°F. Uncover the pot and carefully transfer the cooked lamb shanks to a rimmed baking sheet. Using oven mitts, carefully strain the contents of the pot through a sieve into a clean saucepan. Place the saucepan over medium-high heat and bring to a boil. Continue to boil until the liquid has been reduced by half, 8 to 10 minutes. Remove the pan from the heat, add the butter, and whisk until combined. Adjust the seasoning with salt to your liking.

To serve, remove the warmed lamb shanks from the oven and transfer them to a serving platter. Generously pour the reduced braising liquid over the shanks. Drizzle the yogurt over the top and garnish with the sesame seeds, peanuts, cilantro, mint, and lemon juice. Serve right away.

Pine-Smoked Salmon

MAKES 6 TO 8 SERVINGS

FISH SAUCE GLAZE

½ cup fish sauce, preferably Red Boat brand

½ cup sugar or honey

½ cup fresh lime juice

2 tablespoons rice vinegar

3 Thai chiles, finely chopped

Pine or cedar logs, or charcoal and pine or cedar chips, soaked in water for 10 to 60 minutes

One 4- to 6-pound half side of King salmon, pin bones removed

1 tablespoon fine sea salt

6 shiso sprigs

Leaves from 1 bunch *each* fresh cilantro, dill, and mint

2 tablespoons extra-virgin olive oil

Hot cooked rice, for serving

Lime wedges, for garnish

The bonfire has become a monthly routine since moving to the coast of Mendocino. It is also an experimental environment for cooking different foods over the fire. I first tried this salmon recipe a few months into the Covid-19 pandemic and it quickly became a hit within our friend group. Cooking this dish is a great outdoor group activity that allows for smoke-filled conversations and delicious moist salmon. The key to this cooking technique is to slowly increase the temperature inside the salmon, not to quickly cook the salmon.

To make the glaze, in a saucepan, combine the fish sauce, sugar, lime juice, vinegar, and chiles. Set over medium heat. As soon as the liquid comes to a boil, remove from the heat. Set aside until you are ready to cook the salmon.

Using the logs, build a fire in an outdoor fire pit or charcoal grill. In order to create a balanced heat mass, allow the wood to burn down to coals. Arrange a cooking rack over the coals (I use a metal cooling rack for baking). Or, if using charcoal, the coals should look white and coated with ash.

Season the salmon evenly with salt and place it on the cooking rack away from the coals (you want to cook it over indirect heat). Add small pieces of wood chips over the coals to create a generous stream of smoke. Brush an even layer of the glaze onto the salmon and let it cook until the flesh begins to firm up near the skin, brushing with glaze every 3 to 5 minutes, for 20 to 25 minutes. During this time, the heat should be rising slowly and gradually and there should be no sizzling happening. If you hear sizzling, carefully rotate the grate so that the fillet is positioned further away from the heat.

Strew the herbs over the salmon. Drizzle with the olive oil and continue to cook slowly until the meat gently flakes when you gently press the fish with your finger, 5 to 10 more minutes.

Transfer the salmon to a cutting board. Divide the rice among serving bowls. Using a large serving spoon, spoon pieces of the fish over the rice. Drizzle with a squeeze of lime juice and any remaining glaze.

Pan-Seared Salmon with Summer Succotash

Salmon season on the Mendocino Coast is one of my favorite times of the year. The days begin to grow longer and the harvest from the sea begins to ramp up. For centuries, the king salmon has been a staple food for humans who have inhabited the Mendocino Coast. Every year at the cafe, I pair salmon with a summer vegetable succotash. It is a simple, healthy, and most importantly, delicious way to enjoy salmon.

MAKES 4 SERVINGS

Four 8-ounce skin-on king salmon fillets

Fine sea salt and freshly ground black pepper

1 tablespoon grapeseed oil

2 tablespoons unsalted butter

1 garlic clove, smashed

1 sprig fresh thyme

Summer Succotash (page 244)

Preheat the oven to 400°F.

Season the salmon on both sides with salt and pepper. Place an ovenproof sauté pan over medium-high heat. When hot, add the grapeseed oil and carefully place the salmon in the pan skin side down. It is very important to lay the fish fillets down working away from your body, this will ensure that the oil does not splatter toward you. Once the salmon hits the pan, firmly press down on the fish fillet to ensure the skin is contacting the pan. The skin will want to curl up into a cup shape but continue to press down until the fish stops pushing back toward you. Repeat with the other fillets. Put the pan in the preheated oven and cook for 5 minutes.

Remove the sauté pan from the oven and place it on the stovetop over medium-high heat. Protecting your hand with an oven mitt, (remember, the pan has been in the oven!) add the butter, garlic, and thyme to the pan. Allow the butter to melt and brown. Using a fish spatula, turn the fillets over and baste the fillets with the melted butter mixture. Spoon each fillet with hot butter 5 times (so 20 spoons in total) and then immediately remove the fish from the pan.

To serve, divide the succotash among serving plates and place the cooked salmon on top. Summer on a plate is served.

WARNING

Toulouse Vineyards & Winery

SUPPLIER SPOTLIGHT

After graduating from Gonzaga University in Spokane, Washington, in 2014, I drove the coastal route back home to Los Angeles. Already charmed by Mendocino, my Dad encouraged me to make a pitstop in the small town. This was my first time in Mendocino, and its sleepiness was apparent as soon as I pulled into town off Highway 1. I didn't even bother to stop on Lansing Street, Mendocino's main drag. Instead, I zoomed east toward Anderson Valley because I had heard that it's a superb wine region and my interest in wine was budding. Upon reaching the Valley, I pulled off the road at Toulouse Vineyards & Winery. It was an arbitrary pick among the abundance of winery options along Highway 128. I eagerly popped in for a tasting and was lucky to meet Vern, Toulouse's owner. The wine was fantastic and everyone who worked there seemed to love what they did and where they lived. I knew at that moment that this was a special experience—one that would stay with me for years—even though I couldn't have known that I'd ever return to this area.

Ultimately, when I returned to Mendocino a couple of years later to consider purchasing Cafe Beaujolais, Toulouse was part of my story once again. This time it was my very first meal at the cafe and I deliberately ordered a familiar bottle of wine: Toulouse's Pinot Noir. I remember the choice made me feel somewhat fancy, and I felt a casual elegance wash over me as I sipped the delicious wine and supported a local winery.

Soon thereafter I was buying wine for our restaurant, and I made it my mission to visit every winery in the area in an attempt to forge relationships with the local purveyors. Vern at Toulouse still remembered me two and a half years later. He knew a good relationship with Cafe Beaujolais would bring steady traffic to Toulouse, and our exchanges have multiplied many times over since. In fact, in my first two years of living in Mendocino, I'd stop at Toulouse every time I drove through the valley. Toulouse's employees frequently dine at Beaujolais, and when guests ask for winery recommendations, we send them to Toulouse. Now, Toulouse is the winery that's most represented at the cafe. Whenever I enter the dining room during service, I always see several Toulouse-topped tables, and it gives me the same gratifying feeling I experienced when ordering a bottle with my first Cafe Beaujolais dinner.

Toulouse's light, high-acid wines pair well with food and are never overpowering. At Cafe Beaujolais, we always have duck on the dinner menu and we always have a Toulouse Pinot Noir on the wine list. It's a traditional pairing—the wine's acidity cuts the richness of the duck, and the cherry-like fruit is a pleasing match—and it's a great representation of Anderson Valley. We're also proud to pour their "Goose Bubbles," a small-batch, artisanal sparkling wine that was first released in 2018.

Toulouse stands out from the new age of wineries in the region because Vern Boltz and his wife Maxine value Anderson Valley's essence and culture. They've cultivated the great Alsatian varietals that originally grew in the Valley, such as Riesling, Gewurztraminer, and Pinot Gris, and are a fundamental part of its wine history.

For the full Toulouse Vineyards & Winery experience, we encourage our guests to visit Toulouse's tasting room. I recommend grabbing an outdoor table on the terrace overlooking the beautiful valley, as that's where my personal Toulouse journey began.

Pork Tenderloin with Marsala Sauce

MAKES 4 TO 5 SERVINGS

2 pork tenderloins, 12 to 16 ounces each, silver skin removed

2 tablespoons ras el hanout

1 tablespoon fine sea salt

1 tablespoon extra-virgin olive oil

½ cup Marsala

1 cup Chicken Stock (page 294)

2 tablespoons unsalted butter

Humble pork tenderloin is one of my favorite "proteins" to prepare at the restaurant. It can shine if prepared correctly and seasoned appropriately. I created this recipe at Cafe Beaujolais after my first year at the helm. It is an interesting blend of flavors with Moroccan spices and Marsala wine. The flavors of this dish allow the pork to shine, and it pairs beautifully with sautéed chanterelle mushrooms. The one thing to mention when cooking pork tenderloin is to be careful not to overcook it; the pork should be a blush pink when sliced. Serve with your choice of starch or vegetables.

Preheat the oven to 375°F.

Season the pork tenderloins all over with ras el hanout and salt. Place a large ovenproof cast-iron skillet over medium heat. Add the olive oil. When hot, add the seasoned pork tenderloins and cook until evenly brown on all sides, about 1 minute per side.

Place the pork tenderloins in the preheated oven and roast for 3 minutes. Flip the pork tenderloins and roast until the pork springs back when touched with a finger and feels slightly firm, about 3 more minutes.

Remove the pan from the oven and transfer the pork to a plate to rest. Protecting your hand with an oven mitt (remember, the pan has been in the oven!), place the skillet over high heat. Add the Marsala and cook until the liquid has almost completely evaporated, being sure the alcohol vapors have burned off. Beware that the wine may ignite when added to the hot pan; take extra care to not stand too close to the pan upon adding the Marsala. After about 1 minute, carefully place your head over the pan and smell the sauce. If the alcohol vapor has evaporated in its entirety, you will not be able to smell the alcohol fumes. Add the stock and cook until the liquid has reduced by half and the sauce begins to thicken, about 4 minutes. Add the butter and remove the pan from the heat. Gently swirl the pan; the butter will melt and emulsify into the pan sauce.

To serve, slice the pork on the bias into ½-inch slices. Transfer the slices to a serving platter and pour the Marsala pan sauce over the pork. Serve warm.

Potato Gnocchi

While cooking at a restaurant in Spokane, Washington, while I was attending college, I learned how to make homemade gnocchi. I was technically the pastry cook at the restaurant but could not resist asking questions about techniques and processes about savory dishes, learning things that I would not have picked up unless I let my curiosity wander. I practiced the techniques I learned with my roommates. I hit a home run the first time I made gnocchi for the lot of hungry guys and it became an instant and often requested hit. The most important step in this recipe is to use a proper potato ricer to process the potatoes. Serve with your favorite pasta sauce or with the pesto in this recipe.

MAKES 4 TO 6 SERVINGS

2 pounds russet potatoes, unpeeled

2 cups all-purpose flour, plus more as needed

2 extra-large farm-fresh eggs

2 teaspoons fine sea salt

1 cup Spinach-Basil Pesto (page 132)

24 to 32 strips Lemon Confit (page 292)

24 to 32 grape tomatoes, quartered

Shaved Parmigiano-Reggiano cheese

Pea tendrils, for garnish

Place the potatoes in a large saucepan and add cold water to cover; take care that the potatoes are fully submerged in the water. Set the pan over medium-high heat and bring the water to a simmer. Cook gently until a paring knife can be inserted with little resistance, 20 to 30 minutes. Carefully remove the potatoes from the water and let them cool to room temperature.

When the potatoes are cool, use a paring knife to remove the skin. Run the potatoes through a ricer into a bowl. Add the flour, eggs, and salt to the bowl. Using your hands, work the mixture to incorporate the potatoes with the flour, egg, and salt. You will begin to notice a Play Dough–like consistency: the dough should feel moist and malleable, but not too wet. At this point, take a small piece of dough, form it into a ball, and roll it out into a snake form on a floured surface. If the "snake" is smooth, then the dough is ready. If it feels tacky or sticky, add a bit more flour until a smooth consistency is reached.

Put a large, fresh pot of salted water on the stove over high heat. Fill a large bowl with ice water.

CONTINUED

Potato Gnocchi *(continued)*

Divide the dough into 6 pieces. Working with 1 piece at a time, roll out the dough on a floured work surface, using both hands in tandem to form long, even rope-like pieces of dough. Use a sharp knife to cut the rope into ½-inch pieces and place them onto a floured baking sheet. Continue to roll and cut the dough until all the gnocchi are formed.

When the pot of water is boiling, work in batches by adding 15 to 20 gnocchi to the boiling water and cook until all of the gnocchi in the batch float to the surface, 2 to 3 minutes. Use a spider or sieve to retrieve the gnocchi from the boiling water and place directly into the ice bath. Let the gnocchi sit in the ice bath for 1 minute, then use the spider or sieve to transfer them to an oiled baking sheet. Repeat to cook and chill the remaining gnocchi.

The gnocchi may be used immediately or frozen on the baking sheet. Once frozen, place the cooked gnocchi in locking plastic bags and freeze for up to 3 months. Resting the gnocchi allows the gluten from the flour to rest, which in turn makes the gnocchi more tender.

To reheat, drop the gnocchi into a pot of boiling water and cook until they float once more. Transfer the gnocchi to a large bowl and quickly toss with the pesto until coated. Divide the gnocchi and pesto among serving bowls. Top each bowl with the lemon confit, tomatoes, and shaved Parmesan. Garnish with pea tendrils and serve right away.

CAFE BEAUJOLAIS

Side Food

SIDE FOOD

This chapter highlights a few of my favorite side dishes that I serve at the cafe but also love to serve when I host dinner parties at home. Using fresh, local, organic produce is of the utmost importance in these recipes due to their simplicity. When it comes to most things in the kitchen, my philosophy is "less is more" and these side dishes are no different.

A fun story that I tell many amateur cooks or new hires at the cafe stems from an experience I had while I was cooking in Italy. I showed up for work at a quaint, unassuming osteria in Civitavecchia. At that point in my culinary adventure, my experience with Italian food had been rooted in the American interpretation of Italian cuisine—a heavy use of garlic, onion, tomatoes, and olive oil; and pasta topped with a mountain of cheese and bread crumbs. To my surprise, the Italian food at this restaurant was the exact opposite of my expectations. The chef had one head of garlic on the counter and one onion in his produce bin—both were used in only one dish on the menu. He had a small piece of pecorino romano for the shift, which he used with intent and with restraint. His goal, he told me, was to allow the main ingredient of the dish to shine, whether it be branzino or octopus from the ocean or broccoli rabe or tomatoes from the garden. I learned from him that using the highest-quality and in-season ingredients is the key in creating deliciously flavored recipes. Now, I am not advocating for the abolishment of garlic or cheese in cooking, but am trying to ensure that restraint in the use of these types of strong flavors is a benefit in becoming a skilled chef—or home cook.

Building on the lesson I learned in Italy, I designed these accompaniments to hopefully become "go-to" recipes for your kitchen, whether you are making a meal for a dinner party or just want to fulfill a simple weeknight craving. An accompaniment should be an opportunity for you as a home cook to experiment with different flavor combinations. Feel free to swap out herbs, spices, or vegetables in any of these recipes, just be sure to source the freshest and most in-season ingredients that you have at your disposal. These side dishes are the backbone of a meal and provide support to whatever the main dish might be.

Foraging Mushrooms

SUPPLIER SPOTLIGHT

In my pre-Mendocino life, wild mushrooms were a rare delicacy delivered to restaurant kitchens via overnight FedEx. That all changed within my first week at Cafe Beaujolais when a mushroom forager showed up at the back door with a basket full of mushrooms. I was floored. "Where the heck did you get these?" I asked in astonishment. He revealed nothing. (Foragers' rule #1: NEVER reveal your secret spots.) So, I ventured into the woods on my own, where I quickly discovered the local bounty of edible mushrooms even within a five-minute jaunt from Cafe Beaujolais.

Mendocino is a mushroom paradise. With a consistent rainy season and long periods of foggy days, our mild climate, cool nights, and wet winter season create the perfect setting for a long, productive mushroom season from September to May. The other important factor is that mushrooms live in symbiosis with trees, and Mendocino's white pines, live oaks, and stately redwoods are especially conducive to the proliferation of about 3,000 mushroom varieties, 500 of which are edible.

Cafe Beaujolais purchases around 1,000 pounds of wild mushrooms per year, and I'm still in awe when skilled local foragers show up with thirty pounds at a time. Wherever I had previously used cultivated button mushrooms, I now happily use wild mushrooms. When cooked properly, they add textures and flavors to dishes unlike any other ingredient I know. Plus, wild mushrooms love wine as much as we do.

Like all seasonal produce, wild mushroom varieties drive our menu. Porcini, one of my favorite varieties, are usually the first to pop up beneath the coastal pines, along with lobster mushrooms. Their arrival is our gauge for transitioning from summer to fall, as we replace our summer soup with an autumnal cream of mushroom. Next, chanterelles—both golden and white—show their fluted trumpet caps on steep, north-facing, inland hillsides. Chanterelles have the longest season and are therefore one of the most well-known wild mushrooms. November brings candy caps for our desserts and beverages. When we dehydrate them, the whole block of the town smells intoxicatingly of maple syrup. Come December, we're enjoying yellow feet, hedgehogs, and matsutakes. And then my very favorite, black trumpets, arrive in the late winter. Because they have a remarkably meaty texture and an intense depth of flavor, black trumpets work beautifully with rich wintery cooking. Pig's ears and chicken of the woods, both of which are ideal for soups and mushroom duxelles, grow throughout the extended season. In the spring, we're usually lucky to source the prized morels. And then there are the elusive cauliflower mushrooms—you never know when or where they'll grow, but if you see them when you're out walking, they will stop you in your tracks; these fungi are twice the size of your head! They're a treat to find and a pleasure to eat.

I had no idea that cooking in Mendocino would open me up to the dynamic world of wild mushrooms. It's amazing to connect with the elements of their growth and their unparalleled flavors and textures. Next time you're eating a chanterelle or porcini, hopefully you'll think of Mendocino and the talented foragers who spotted them for your delight.

North African Turmeric Rice

MAKES 2 TO 3 SERVINGS

- 1 cup long-grain basmati rice
- 1 tablespoon coconut oil or clarified butter
- 1 shallot, finely minced
- 3 garlic cloves, minced
- 1-inch knob fresh ginger, peeled, smashed, and chopped
- 1 tablespoon fine sea salt
- 1 tablespoon ground turmeric
- 1 teaspoon ground cumin
- ½ teaspoon ground cinnamon
- ¼ cup golden raisins
- ¼ cup shelled pistachios, toasted (see page 295)
- 2 tablespoons tamarind paste
- 1 mandarin orange, washed and quartered
- 1 bay leaf
- 1½ cups low-sodium vegetable broth or water
- 1 bunch fresh cilantro, chopped, for garnish

This recipe packs a surprising amount of flavor. The mandarin orange, used peel and all, provides a delicious sweet and savory touch to counteract the bold spice mix used here. Serve this with grilled vegetables, grilled chicken, braised meats, or enjoy it on its own.

Put the rice in a large mesh strainer and rinse thoroughly under cold water while shaking vigorously. This process helps release the starch particles present on the rice grains. Repeat the rinsing and shaking two to three times, until the water running through the rice runs clear. Set aside.

Warm a sauté pan over medium-low heat. Add the coconut oil, shallot, garlic, ginger, and salt and cook until the garlic and ginger becomes fragrant, about 2 minutes. Stir in the turmeric, cumin, and cinnamon and cook for 2 minutes to dissipate the rawness of the spices. Turn the burner off. Add the raisins, pistachios, tamarind paste, quartered oranges, bay leaf, rinsed rice and broth or water. Thoroughly mix the ingredients in the pan until the liquid begins to turn orange, 15 to 30 seconds. Transfer the contents of the pot to a rice cooker and cook according to the manufacturer's instructions on the standard white rice setting. After the rice finishes cooking, let it rest for about 10 minutes in the cooker.

Remove the bay leaf. Fluff the rice grains gently with a fork. Transfer the rice to a platter and sprinkle with chopped cilantro. Serve warm.

Southern Indian Coconut Rice

While traveling in Thailand and Singapore, I was exposed to some amazing coconut rice. This recipe is inspired by the rice that I was served in many street food stalls from those travels, but I take it to the next level by adding the spices of Indian cuisine. The coconut milk provides an amazing richness to the rice and is an upgrade from using plain water. This rice works wonderfully with curries and packs enough flavor to stand up on its own. The pickled shallots and fresh herbs provide acidity to counter the richness of the coconut milk. Look for asafoetida and fenugreek seeds, elements of curry powder blends, at an Indian food store or from an online source.

MAKES 4 TO 6 SERVINGS

PICKLED SHALLOTS

2 cups water

½ cup red wine vinegar

2 tablespoons granulated sugar

1 teaspoon fine sea salt

2 shallots, sliced at a diagonal into thin strands

2 cups ice cubes

COCONUT RICE

2 cups long-grain basmati rice

1 tablespoon coconut oil or clarified butter

3 garlic cloves, minced

1 stalk lemongrass, crushed and finely minced

1 tablespoon fine sea salt

1 tablespoon whole yellow mustard seeds

1 whole dried chile, such as chile de arbol, seeds removed

1 teaspoon fenugreek seeds

½ teaspoon asafoetida

4 curry leaves, torn (optional)

1 cup coconut flakes, lightly toasted (see page 295)

2 tablespoons lime zest

1⅓ cups canned unsweetened coconut milk

1 cup low-sodium vegetable broth or water

1 cup peanuts, toasted (see page 295) and crushed

½ cup fresh mint leaves, roughly torn

Leaves from 1 bunch fresh cilantro, chopped, for garnish

Juice of 2 limes

To make the pickled shallots, in a saucepan, combine the water, vinegar, sugar, and salt and bring to a rolling boil over high heat. Add the sliced shallots and then immediately turn the burner off and add the ice cubes. Let the shallots stand in the liquid for at least 15 minutes or up to 2 weeks in an airtight container. Drain the shallots through a fine-mesh sieve.

To make the coconut rice, put the rice in a large mesh strainer and rinse thoroughly under cold water while shaking vigorously. This process helps release the starch particles present on the rice grain. Repeat the rinsing and shaking two to three times, until the water running through the rice runs clear. Set aside.

Warm a sauté pan over medium-low heat. Add the coconut oil, garlic, lemongrass, salt, mustard seed, dried chile, fenugreek seeds, and asafoetida, to the pan and cook, stirring with a wooden spoon, for 2 minutes to dissipate the rawness of the vegetables and spices. Turn off the burner. Add the curry leaves (if using), ½ cup of the coconut flakes, the lime zest, rinsed rice, coconut milk, and broth and mix thoroughly. Transfer the contents of the pot to a rice cooker and cook according to the manufacturer's instructions on the standard white rice setting. After the rice finishes cooking, let it rest for about 10 minutes in the cooker.

To serve, open the rice cooker and fluff the rice grains with a fork. Transfer the rice to a large serving bowl and top with the toasted peanuts, pickled shallots, remaining ½ cup toasted coconut flakes, and fresh herbs. Squeeze the lime juice over the top and serve warm.

Pesto Rice

MAKES 3 TO 4 SERVINGS

1 cup jasmine rice, rinsed

3 cloves garlic, smashed

½ teaspoon red pepper flakes

1 tablespoon fine sea salt

Finely grated zest of 1 lemon

1 cup ice cold water

¼ cup fresh lemon juice, plus the juice of ½ lemon

¾ cup untoasted blanched slivered almonds

½ cup extra-virgin olive oil, plus more for drizzling

4 cups loosely packed baby spinach

½ cup loosely packed fresh basil leaves, plus fresh basil ribbons for garnish

1 teaspoon baking soda

Having The Brickery attached to the Cafe allows me to swap ingredients from the two locations with ease. This recipe came about when I needed to pair a starch dish with some chicken breast from the Cafe. This pesto rice has a fair amount of acidity from the fresh lemon juice that allows the rice to pop with freshness. I recommend making this when you need a side dish to pair with grilled vegetables or chicken.

Put the rice in a large mesh strainer and rinse thoroughly under cold water while shaking vigorously. This process helps release the starch particles present on the rice grain. Repeat the rinsing and shaking two to three times, until the water running through the rice runs clear. Set aside.

In a blender, combine the garlic, red pepper flakes, salt, lemon zest, water, ¼ cup lemon juice, ½ cup of the almonds, the olive oil, spinach, basil, and baking soda. Blend on high speed until the mixture resembles a green smoothie. (It's important to work quickly and keep the ingredients as cold as possible to maintain a vibrant green color.)

Pour the rinsed rice and pesto puree into a rice cooker and cook according to the manufacturer's instructions on the standard white rice setting. After the rice finishes cooking, let it rest for about 10 minutes in the cooker.

To serve, fluff the rice grains with a fork. Transfer the rice to a serving platter and sprinkle with basil ribbons, the remaining ¼ cup almonds, the juice of ½ lemon, and a light drizzle of oil. Serve warm.

Classic Polenta

CLASSIC
BEAUJOLAIS

Most recipes indicate a far shorter cooking time for making polenta, but it never seems done enough to me at that point; I'm still aware of the mouthfeel of gritty, individual grains. I love how tender and almost fluffy it is after just 45 seconds reheated in the microwave. Polenta is a foil to many preparations, as a base for Black Bean Chili (page 103) or a hearty beef or mushroom ragu. It's also satisfying topped with garlicky sautéed vegetables. Be sure to plate the polenta so that its bright yellow is visible—it makes the finished dish pop. —MF

MAKES 6 SERVINGS

- 5 cups water
- 2 teaspoons kosher salt, plus more as needed
- 1 cup dried polenta
- 2 cups fresh or frozen corn kernels
- 3 tablespoons unsalted butter (optional)
- 1 cup freshly grated Parmigiano-Reggiano cheese (optional)
- 1 cup grapeseed or canola oil (optional)
- Chopped fresh parsley, for garnish (optional)

For soft polenta, in a heavy-bottomed saucepan, bring the water to a boil over high heat. Stir in the salt, then while whisking vigorously, slowly pour in the polenta. Reduce the heat to medium-low and keep stirring. At a certain point, the polenta will start to spit—avoid letting it hit your skin (think "molten lava"). Cover the pan and continue to cook for 30 minutes, stirring every 5 to 10 minutes. Stir in the corn and continue to cook until the polenta is thick and smooth and no longer gritty, another 10 minutes. Stir in the butter and/or cheese, if desired, and serve right away.

For firm polenta, lightly oil the sides and bottom of a 9 by 13-inch baking pan. Pour in the prepared soft polenta and spread it out with a spatula. Let it chill in the refrigerator for 2 hours. Cut into serving portions and reheat in a microwave on the high setting for 20 to 30 seconds.

For fried polenta, follow the instructions for firm polenta up to cutting the polenta into serving portions. Place a high-sided frying pan over medium-low heat and add 1 cup grapeseed or canola oil. Gradually warm the oil until it registers 300°F on an instant-read thermometer. When hot, working in batches to prevent crowding, place the polenta pieces into the pan and cook until golden, flipping halfway through, 2 to 3 minutes. Transfer the polenta to a metal cooling rack or paper towel to drain. Season with salt, sprinkle with parsley, if desired, and enjoy.

MODERN BEAUJOLAIS

Dashi Polenta

MAKES 4 SERVINGS

DASHI

4½ cups water

One 4-inch square piece dried kombu

1 cup katsuobushi (dried bonito flakes)

1 cup dry polenta

1 teaspoon fine sea salt

4 tablespoons unsalted butter

Dashi is a staple in Japanese cooking. It adds complexity, salinity, and umami to any food that it comes in contact with. I decided to include this in my cookbook due to the uniqueness and deliciousness of the final product. The cooking technique is very similar to how Margaret cooks her polenta, but the flavors are very different. I do believe it is a perfect comparison to see how her flavors differ from my own. Traditional Italian polenta is an ultimate pairing with braised meat dishes or roasted mushrooms. This dish differs due to the umami richness that the dashi brings to the polenta. I recommend pairing this with grilled seasonal vegetables, lighter proteins, even salmon! Make both recipes at home and see for yourself.

In a saucepan, combine the water and kombu and allow to steep for 2 to 4 hours. This allows the kombu to gently release its flavor into the water without the use of heat.

Place the saucepan over medium-low heat and gently bring the water to a simmer. As soon as the water begins to bubble, remove the kombu from the water and add the katsuobushi. Gently bring the water back to a simmer and set the timer for 30 seconds. Turn the heat off and allow the mixture to steep for 10 minutes.

Strain the dashi into a clean saucepan and bring to a boil over high heat. While whisking, slowly add the polenta and the salt and reduce the heat to low. Slowly cook the polenta, whisking frequently. Once the mixture becomes too thick for a whisk, change to a wooden spoon for stirring. Cook until the polenta is thick and smooth, 15 to 20 minutes. Stir in the butter until melted. Serve right away.

Mexican-Style Street Corn

Mexican street corn, also known as elotes, is one of the great salty, savory pleasures you can enjoy in Mexico. I came up with this recipe in an attempt to try and recreate those delicious flavors in the dining room of Cafe Beaujolais. I recommend trying this recipe during the summer months when corn is abundant in the market. I think I came fairly close to my goal and I hope you will agree.

MAKES 8 SERVINGS

8 ears fresh corn, husks removed

1 tablespoon grapeseed oil, plus more for greasing corn

1 teaspoon fine sea salt

2 cloves garlic, minced

4 tablespoons unsalted butter, cut into cubes

Leaves from 1 bunch fresh cilantro

4 tablespoons crème fraîche

½ cup crumbled queso fresco

1 teaspoon Aleppo pepper flakes

Heat an outdoor grill over medium heat or preheat your oven's broiler until hot.

Rub the corn ears with grapeseed oil and season evenly with salt. Grill the corn, turning it as it cooks, until evenly browned on all sides, 2 to 3 minutes per side. Transfer the corn to a metal rack to cool.

Using a large knife, cut the kernels from the cob into a bowl.

Warm a large cast-iron skillet over medium-high heat. Add 1 tablespoon grapeseed oil and the minced garlic. Cook until the garlic just begins to brown, about 30 seconds, then add the browned corn kernels. Sauté just to heat the corn through, about 1 minute. Add the cubed butter and fold into the corn until the butter melts. Transfer the corn to a bowl and top with cilantro, crème fraîche, queso fresco, and Aleppo pepper. Serve warm.

Summer Succotash

MAKES 4 SERVINGS

- 2 tablespoons extra-virgin olive oil
- 4 zucchinis, cut into ½-inch cubes
- 1 teaspoon fine sea salt
- 1 teaspoon freshly cracked black pepper
- Kernels from 4 ears fresh corn
- 4 cloves garlic, minced
- 1 shallot, finely chopped
- One 10-ounce jar piquillo peppers, drained and cut into ⅛-inch slices
- Leaves from 1 bunch flat-leaf parsley, finely chopped
- Juice of ½ lemon
- 2 tablespoons butter

During the summer months we are inundated at the restaurant with copious amounts of zucchini and corn. We use the zucchini in cakes, breads, pastas, pizzas, grilled, baked, and steamed but still seem to have more. I developed this succotash as another way to use the summer bounty. It is a recipe that goes great with salmon (see page 215) or as a side for a summer barbecue.

Warm a large cast-iron skillet over medium-high heat. Add the olive oil, zucchini, salt, and pepper and sauté until the zucchini begins to brown slightly, 3 to 5 minutes. Add the corn, garlic, and shallot and cook until the corn is tender, 5 to 10 minutes, stirring occasionally. Add the piquillo peppers, parsley, lemon juice, and butter. Turn off heat and fold the butter into the succotash until the butter is melted. Serve warm.

Potato Goop

CLASSIC BEAUJOLAIS

I remember these potatoes from the early 80s when I was cooking dinner. Many people over the years have proclaimed this recipe their favorite with a dreamy look in their eyes. Testing it again, I know why—these potatoes are frighteningly irresistible. The long baking period allows the coating to permeate the vegetable. I didn't try it but imagine you could use this mixture to make a dynamite garlic bread or toast. —MF

MAKES 4 SERVINGS

3 tablespoons plus 1 teaspoon kosher salt

3¼ pounds red potatoes, on the smaller side, unpeeled

1 dried bay leaf (use 2, if small)

¼ teaspoon finely ground black pepper

⅓ cup olive oil

3 cloves garlic

4 shallots, coarsely chopped

½ cup chopped fresh parsley

1 teaspoon fresh thyme leaves

½ cup unsalted butter, melted

Bring a large pot of water to a boil and add 3 tablespoons of the salt.

Add the potatoes to the water along with the bay leaf and boil until just tender, 15 to 20 minutes, depending on size. Drain the potatoes, cool them, and refrigerate them for at least 3 hours or overnight.

Preheat the oven to 350°F. Cut the potatoes into quarters.

In the bowl of a food processor, combine the remaining 1 teaspoon salt, the pepper, olive oil, garlic, shallots, parsley, and thyme and process until finely chopped. Transfer to a bowl, stir in the melted butter, then pour this mixture over the potatoes. Mix the potato-herb mixture with a flat-bottomed spatula, scooping from the bottom in order to coat the potatoes well on all sides. Transfer the potatoes to a 9 by 13-inch or 10 by 15-inch baking pan, spreading them out in a single layer. Bake until the potatoes are crispy, turning them periodically with the spatula, about 2 hours. Serve warm.

Roasted Baby Beets with Pecorino and Fresh Mint

MAKES 4 SERVINGS

4 bunches baby beets, leaves and stalks removed, scrubbed well and patted dry

1 teaspoon fine sea salt

4 tablespoons extra-virgin olive oil

½ cup grated pecorino romano cheese

1 bunch fresh mint, chopped, plus small whole mint leaves for garnish, optional

Some people claim that beets taste like the earth and shy away from eating them, while others enjoy the earthy taste. If you're among those who do not enjoy beets' dirtlike flavor, I would argue that you're missing out on a fantastic treat and urge you to try them again. Look for the freshest beets at the market. Also, when shopping at your local farmers market or organic grocer, try to find the smaller, baby beets, with the leaves on, which is a marker of freshness. This recipe highlights the beautiful simplicity of tender baby beets, which allows their sweetness to shine through simple roasting.

Preheat the oven to 350°F.

Place the beets into a large bowl and toss with the salt and 2 tablespoons of the oil until well coated. Wrap each beet individually with aluminum foil. Place the wrapped beets on a baking sheet and place into the preheated oven. Bake until the tip of a paring knife inserted into the largest beet meets very little resistance, 30 to 45 minutes. Remove from the oven and let cool until the beets are cool enough to handle, about 10 minutes.

Carefully unwrap the foil from the beets, cut into slices, and place onto a serving platter. Sprinkle with the pecorino cheese and mint, and finish with the drizzle of extra-virgin olive oil and whole mint leaves, if desired. Serve warm.

Herbed Fingerling Potatoes with Crème Fraîche

MODERN BEAUJOLAIS

If you want to impress your guests with an out-of-the-park delicious side dish, this is the one. I have been wowing guests at the cafe with this for years. Twice-cooking the potatoes is the key to their crisp texture.

MAKES 4 SERVINGS

- ½ cup olive oil
- 5 cloves garlic, crushed
- 1 pound fingerling potatoes
- 3 tablespoons fine sea salt
- ½ cup crème fraîche
- 1 bunch fresh chives, finely chopped
- 1 teaspoon freshly cracked black pepper

Put the olive oil in a small saucepan and set over medium heat. Warm the olive oil for 2 minutes. Place the crushed garlic into the hot oil, then remove the saucepan from the heat. Set aside.

Place the potatoes in a large pot and cover with cold water by 1 inch. Add the salt, set over high heat, and bring the water to a boil. Boil the potatoes until they are tender when pierced with a small knife, 15 to 20 minutes. Drain the potatoes well, then transfer to a rimmed baking sheet and allow to cool until cool enough to touch, about 15 minutes. Meanwhile, preheat the oven to 375°F.

Using the palm of your hand, gently smash the potatoes on the baking sheet, taking care that they do not break apart. Remove the garlic cloves from the oil and pour the oil onto the baking sheet with the potatoes. Using a spatula, gently move the potatoes around, allowing the oil to seep under the smashed potatoes. Bake until the potatoes begin to brown and crisp, about 20 minutes.

Transfer the potatoes to a paper towel–lined plate briefly to drain the excess oil, then arrange them on a serving platter. Drizzle the potatoes with the crème fraîche and top with chopped chives and freshly cracked black pepper.

Roasted Carrots with Dukkah and Mint Yogurt Sauce

MAKES 4 SMALL SERVINGS

DUKKAH SPICE BLEND

2 tablespoons whole almonds

1 tablespoon sesame seeds

½ teaspoon fennel seeds

½ teaspoon cumin seeds

½ teaspoon coriander seeds

¼ teaspoon cayenne pepper

1 pound baby carrots, peeled, or regular carrots, peeled and cut into 1-inch pieces

2 tablespoons olive oil

1 teaspoon fine sea salt

MINT YOGURT SAUCE

1 cup plain Greek yogurt

¼ cup fresh mint leaves, roughly chopped

1 garlic clove, minced

Juice of 1 lemon

The North African spices in this recipe lend themselves especially well to the natural sweetness of carrots. The easy yogurt sauce flavored with fresh mint and garlic is a wonderful complement to the spices. This side dish is versatile, as it can either be served hot straight out of the oven or can be enjoyed at room temperature.

Preheat the oven to 375°F and place a rimmed metal baking sheet on the center rack of the oven.

To make the dukkah, while the oven preheats, place a cast iron pan or a heavy-bottomed sauté pan over medium heat and add the whole almonds. Toast the almonds until some color begins to develop, 1 to 2 minutes. Remove the nuts from the pan and pour onto a plate or bowl to stop the cooking. Place the pan back over the heat and add the sesame, fennel, cumin, and coriander seeds and toast until some color begins to develop and the seeds are fragrant, 1 to 2 minutes. Remove from the heat and pour onto the plate with the almonds.

Transfer the toasted ingredients and cayenne to the bowl of a food processor and process until the spice mixture looks like wet sand, 30 to 40 seconds. Transfer the spice blend to a small bowl and set aside.

Place the carrots, olive oil, and salt into a medium bowl and toss to ensure every carrot is coated with oil. Place the carrots onto the preheated baking sheet and bake until the carrots are browned in places and a fork inserted into the center of the largest carrot glides through with minimal resistance, 15 to 20 minutes. Remove the carrots from the oven and transfer back into the mixing bowl. Add the dukkah spice blend and toss to coat. Keep warm.

To make the Mint Yogurt Sauce, in a small bowl, combine the yogurt, mint, garlic, and lemon juice and mix until blended.

To serve, spread the yogurt mixture onto a serving platter and place the cooked, dukkah-seasoned carrots over the yogurt mixture. Serve hot or at room temperature.

Desserts

DESSERTS

I discovered my love for the culinary arts at the age of fourteen. The first recipe I adapted as my own was for lemon cheesecake. I excitedly shared my rendition with family and friends, and they encouraged me to create a small business selling the tangy cakes. As the silent partner at an Italian restaurant in Long Beach, my dad introduced me and my lemon cheesecake to the restaurant owner. After that, twice a week, I'd go to the restaurant, bake some cheesecakes, and get paid under the table. Over time, I improved the recipe, making homemade Graham crackers for the crust and substituting crème fraîche for sour cream. Now the very best version of my original, almost twenty-year-old lemon cheesecake recipe is on the Cafe Beaujolais dessert menu. Oozing in comfort, while using high-quality ingredients, it's the baseline for the classic style of desserts we make at the Cafe.

My former cheesecake business notwithstanding, I'm mostly a savory chef. I've approached Beaujolais's dessert menu by honoring its past. Former owner Margaret Fox was a legendary baker, and people often came to the restaurant specifically for her desserts. Fortunately, Margaret left a huge box of laminated recipe cards featuring everything Cafe Beaujolais served in her twenty-two years in business. The fact that she documented all these recipes was impressive, and now they are in my hands so that I can recreate the joy her desserts brought to Beaujolais customers for two decades.

Margaret's coconut cream pie and gingerbread cake were best sellers that people associated with the restaurant. I tweaked the latter only slightly, adding more zing with fresh and candied ginger in addition to the ground spice. The ice cream base that we now use is courtesy of Chef Chris Kump, and I'm beyond grateful for it. It's the best, creamiest ice cream, so being able to share it in this book is really exciting. Of course, we've made it our own by incorporating local flavors, such as mint, the latter which you'll find a recipe for in these pages as well.

The dessert recipes we've adopted from Margaret's days are tried and true and are still a hit forty years since their creation. While some bakers search for over-the-top elaborate desserts, we aim for simpler techniques and guaranteed satisfaction. Happy baking!

Cast-Iron Gingerbread

MAKES ONE 10- TO 12-INCH CAKE

- ¾ cup unsalted butter, softened, plus more for greasing
- ¾ cup firmly packed dark brown sugar
- ¾ cup molasses
- 2 large farm-fresh eggs, at room temperature
- ½ teaspoon fine sea salt
- 1½ cups all-purpose flour
- 2 teaspoons ground ginger
- 2 teaspoons baking soda
- ¾ cup buttermilk, at room temperature
- ¾ cup grated fresh ginger
- ½ cup chopped candied ginger
- Vanilla Ice Cream (page 281), for serving

This recipe, a Beaujolais staple for many years, highlights ginger in three different forms: ground ginger, freshly grated ginger, and candied ginger. We serve this dessert in personal-sized cast-iron skillets to show off the dessert's casual and homestyle character. Great food generally doesn't need to be avant-garde, it just needs to taste delicious and provide a nostalgic feeling. We generally like to serve warmed desserts during the colder months of the year. To grate this large quantity of fresh ginger, I recommend using the food processor's grater attachment. If you don't own a food processor, use some elbow grease and grate the ginger with a box grater.

Preheat the oven to 350°F. Grease a 10- to 12-inch cast-iron skillet with butter.

In a stand mixer fitted with the paddle attachment, or in a bowl, combine the butter and brown sugar. Beat on medium speed, or with a hand whisk, until the mixture is light and fluffy, about 2 minutes. Add the molasses, eggs, and salt and continue to mix until smooth.

In a separate bowl, whisk together the flour, ground ginger, and baking soda, making sure there are no lumps.

Using a rubber spatula, gently fold half of the flour mixture into the butter mixture, then fold in half of the buttermilk. Repeat these steps until the mixture is smooth and well mixed. Stir in the fresh ginger and candied ginger until well dispersed in the mixture.

Pour the batter into the prepared skillet. Bake until the center is springy and the cake looks set, 30 to 35 minutes. Let the cake rest for 10 to 15 minutes before serving.

Cut the cake into wedges and serve warm with ice cream.

Coconut Cream Pie

MAKES ONE 9-INCH PIE

CRUST

Neutral-flavored cooking spray

1 tablespoon unsalted butter, at room temperature

6 tablespoons sugar

1½ cups unsweetened desiccated coconut

2 ounces bittersweet chocolate (preferably 70%), melted (see page 293)

½ teaspoon fine sea salt

FILLING

3 large egg yolks

2 cups unsweetened coconut milk

½ cup sugar

3 tablespoons cornstarch

1 teaspoon fine sea salt

⅔ cup unsweetened desiccated coconut

1 tablespoon coconut extract

GARNISH

1 cup cold heavy whipping cream

¼ cup powdered sugar

¾ cup unsweetened flaked coconut, toasted (see page 295)

This recipe has been a constant on the dessert menu of Cafe Beaujolais. It was developed nearly forty years ago when Margaret Fox owned the cafe and has not changed since.

To make the crust, preheat the oven to 325°F. Lightly coat a 9-inch pie pan with cooking spray.

In a bowl, combine the butter and sugar. Using a whisk, beat by hand until well blended. Add the coconut, chocolate, and salt and mix well. Press the mixture into the bottom and up the sides of the prepared pie pan. Bake the crust until firm and lightly browned, 18 to 20 minutes. Remove from the oven and let cool to room temperature.

To make the filling, put the egg yolks in a heatproof bowl and set aside. In a saucepan, whisk together the coconut milk, sugar, cornstarch, and salt. Set on the stove top over medium-high heat and bring the mixture to a boil, whisking constantly and taking care not to scorch the mixture. Boil the mixture until it is noticeably thickened, about 2 minutes, and then remove the saucepan from the heat. While constantly and vigorously whisking, pour one-fourth of the hot coconut milk mixture into the bowl with the egg yolks until blended. Return the egg yolks and coconut milk mixture back to the saucepan and place back over medium-high heat. While whisking constantly, cook until bubbles form around the edges of the saucepan and the mixture thickens, about 1 minute.

Pour the filling through a fine-mesh sieve into a clean bowl. Using a rubber spatula, fold in the desiccated coconut and coconut extract. Let the mixture stand at room temperature for about 15 minutes to cool.

Pour the cooled mixture into the pre-baked pie crust. Refrigerate the pie for at least 4 hours, or preferably overnight.

When ready to serve, remove the pie from the refrigerator. Using a stand mixer or electric mixer with the whisk attachment, whip the cream with the powdered sugar, starting on medium-low speed and slowly increasing the speed until medium peaks form, 3 to 4 minutes. Top the pie with the whipped cream: Using an offset spatula, smooth the whipped cream over the pie to create a nice mound. (Tip: Warm the offset spatula under warm running water, dry with a towel, and then run it over the cream. It will create a smooth texture with an elevated look.) Garnish the top with toasted coconut.

Cut the pie into wedges to serve. (You can also make this pie ahead of time. Wrapped tightly, it will last for 3 days in the refrigerator.)

Lemon Cheesecake

MAKES ONE 9-INCH CAKE

CRUST

2 cups graham cracker crumbs

½ cup unsalted butter, plus more for greasing

FILLING

24 ounces cream cheese, at room temperature

½ cup sugar

3 large farm-fresh eggs, at room temperature

1 tablespoon finely grated lemon zest

½ cup fresh lemon juice

Seeds scraped from 1 vanilla bean

1 teaspoon fine sea salt

TOPPING

1½ cups sour cream or crème fraîche

3 tablespoons sugar

1 teaspoon vanilla extract

LEMON CURD

Zest from 3 lemons, grated with a Microplane or potato peeler

1 cup sugar

4 large farm-fresh eggs

½ cup fresh lemon juice

½ teaspoon fine sea salt

½ cup unsalted butter, at room temperature

My first time cooking—well, baking—was when I was thirteen years old. At this young age, I started a casual business selling cheesecakes to family friends and a local restaurant. This lemony cheesecake with a graham cracker crust and sour cream topping is the recipe that jump-started my cooking career. It may not seem simple, but the extra steps taken will ensure a delicious, creamy dessert that I can guarantee you will want to make again and again. Following are some essential techniques for a great cheesecake. First, you want your ingredients to be at room temperature. This ensures that the cheesecake does not form cracks and it helps the cheesecake cook evenly. Next, fully mix the cream cheese and sugar before you add the eggs. This technique is important in achieving the perfect creamy, smooth texture in the final cake. Finally, allow the cooked cheesecake to come to room temperature before placing it in the refrigerator. This will also help prevent cracking due to gradual cooling of the cake.

To make the crust, preheat the oven to 350°F. Generously butter a 9-inch springform pan. (This is an important step, as the butter is used as a glue to hold the graham cracker crumbs.)

Put the graham cracker crumbs in a bowl. Melt the ½ cup butter in a saucepan over medium heat. Pour the melted butter over the crumbs and mix well. The mixture will resemble wet sand.

Using the back of a spoon, evenly press the graham cracker mixture up to ½ inch from the top of the pan sides of the springform pan, making sure to coat all around. Once the sides are finished, use the remaining mixture to coat the pan bottom. Place the springform pan into the oven and bake until the graham crackers smell toasted, 7 to 10 minutes. Remove from the oven and allow to cool. Leave the oven set to 350°F.

To make the filling, combine the cream cheese and sugar in the bowl of a stand mixer fitted with the paddle attachment. Beat the mixture on medium speed until the mixture is smooth and has no visible chunks of cream cheese, about 2 minutes. Use a rubber spatula to scrape down the sides of the bowl and mix again to blend the ingredients. With the mixer running on medium-low speed, add the eggs, 1 one at a time, being sure that the mixture is homogeneous before adding the next one. Remove the bowl from the stand and use the rubber spatula to gently fold in the lemon zest, lemon juice, vanilla bean seeds, and salt. Pour the mixture into the crust and bake until the cheesecake wobbles slightly in the center when shaken, about 35 minutes.

Meanwhile, make the topping: In a bowl, combine the sour cream, sugar, and vanilla extract and whisk to blend.

Carefully remove the cheesecake from the oven and pour the sour cream topping over the top. Place the cake back in the oven and bake for 15 minutes.

Remove the cheesecake from the oven and let it stand at room temperature for at least 1 hour and up to 2 hours. Once cooled, begin making the lemon curd.

For the lemon curd, place the lemon zest and sugar into a food processor and blend for 1 minute. Add the eggs and pulse a couple times until the eggs are blended into the butter mixture. Using a rubber spatula transfer the sugar and egg mixture into a medium saucepan. Add the lemon juice and salt. With a whisk in hand, turn the burner on medium low heat and begin whisking the mixture. Increase the heat and whisk until the liquid begins to thicken. Once thickened, whisk in the room temperature butter. Strain the curd through a fine-mesh strainer into a clean container.

Pour the warm curd over the cooled cheesecake. Place the cheesecake into the refrigerator for a minimum of 8 hours and up to 3 days.

To serve, cut the cheesecake into 10 wedges.

Amazon Chocolate Cake

CLASSIC
BEAUJOLAIS

Long before we so wholeheartedly embraced vegan foods, this cake delighted people with its magical simplicity. Lacking the rich ingredients commonly thought of as key to a classic version—eggs! butter! dairy!—it's somehow transformed into a satisfying cake. Some kids who were fans in the early days when I first owned Cafe Beaujolais are now grandparents (!) who've told me that this beloved recipe has been their family's birthday cake for three generations. It's a legacy I'm proud of. There is a world of difference in this cake between done and overdone, which can take place within a 5-minute period, so really pay attention during baking. —MF

MAKES ONE 9-INCH CAKE

Cooking spray for greasing pan

1½ cups all-purpose flour (stir before spooning into measuring cup)

⅓ cup unsweetened Dutch process cocoa powder

1 teaspoon baking soda (measure, then sift to remove any lumps)

1 cup granulated sugar

½ teaspoon fine sea salt

1 cup strong brewed coffee, chilled

⅓ cup rice bran oil

1½ teaspoons vanilla extract

1 tablespoon distilled white vinegar

Sweetened whipped cream or a vegan alternative, for serving

Preheat the oven to 350°F. Position the rack in the center of the oven. Line a 9-inch round cake pan with parchment paper and grease the sides with cooking spray.

In a bowl, mix together the flour, cocoa, baking soda, sugar, and sea salt until well blended. In a separate bowl, measure the coffee, oil, vanilla, and white vinegar and stir until blended. Pour the coffee mixture into the flour mixture and stir until just blended. There will be lumps, so strain through a fine-mesh sieve into another bowl and stir briefly to blend. (Don't avoid the straining step because if you instead decide to beat the lumps out of the batter, the cake will be tough.) Pour the batter into the prepared pan and tap the pan on the counter a few times to pop any air bubbles. Place the pan on the middle oven rack and bake until a toothpick inserted into the center of the cake comes out clean, 25 to 30 minutes.

Transfer the cake to a wire rack and run a knife or spatula around the outside to prevent it from sticking. Let cool in the pan for 20 minutes, then turn it out: Place another rack on top and flip it over, so the cake is right side up. Let cool to room temperature

Cut into 8 slices and serve with whipped cream.

MODERN
BEAUJOLAIS

Chocolate Lava Cakes

MAKES 8 CAKES

GANACHE

8 ounces dark chocolate (75% or more) chunks

1 cup heavy whipping cream

½ cup unsalted butter, cut into small chunks

CAKES

Butter for greasing

1 pound dark chocolate (75% or more), chopped

2 cups unsalted butter, melted

6 large farm-fresh eggs, separated

½ teaspoon cream of tartar

¾ cup cornstarch

½ cup sugar

½ teaspoon baking powder

Vanilla Ice Cream (page 281), for serving

These cakes, with a melty chocolate middle, are a hit for special occasions such as anniversary dinners, Valentine's Day dinner, or just simple date nights. The use of high-quality dark chocolate is key to their success. Be careful not to overbake the cakes as the allure and wow factor is to have that flowing "lava" effect. There will be a small amount of ganache leftover. Save it as a snack for later or freeze it in a locking plastic bag for the next time you use this recipe. It will last for up to 6 months in the freezer.

To make the ganache, place a heatproof bowl over (not touching) a saucepan filled with barely simmering water. Add the chocolate and heavy cream to the top bowl. Let the chocolate melt, then whisk it with the cream. Add the butter chunks and whisk until smooth. Pour the mixture onto a small, rimmed baking sheet and place in the refrigerator to cool and become firm, about 2 hours, or overnight.

Remove the baking pan from the refrigerator and cut the firmed ganache into 2 tablespoon chunks.

To make the cakes, preheat the oven to 350°F. Generously grease eight 2-inch ramekins with butter.

Place a clean heatproof bowl over (not touching) a saucepan filled with barely simmering water. Add the chocolate and butter to the bowl and melt them together, whisking until smooth.

In a stand mixer fitted with the whisk attachment, beat the egg whites and cream of tartar on high speed until stiff peaks form, 4 to 5 minutes; set aside. In another bowl, using a rubber spatula, mix the melted chocolate and butter with the cornstarch, egg yolks, sugar, and baking powder. Using a rubber spatula, carefully fold one-fourth of the stiff egg whites into the chocolate mixture until incorporated. Then, carefully fold in the remaining egg whites, trying not to deflate the mixture.

Using an ice cream scoop, portion ½ cup of the batter into each of the ramekins. Bake for 15 minutes. Remove the cakes from the oven and push a chunk of ganache into the center of each cake. Bake until the outer edge of the cake is firm and slightly cracked but the center is still moist and loose, 5 more minutes.

Remove the cakes from the oven and let cool slightly. Unmold the cakes from the ramekins and serve with a generous scoop of ice cream.

CLASSIC
BEAUJOLAIS

Mascarpone Berry Tart (aka Fancy Pants Forgiveness Tart)

MAKES ONE 9-INCH TART

TART DOUGH

2 cups all-purpose flour

¼ cup sugar

¼ teaspoon fine sea salt

Finely grated zest of 1 organic lemon

1 cup cold unsalted butter, cut into 12 pieces total

MASCARPONE FILLING

8 ounces mascarpone

1 teaspoon vanilla extract

1 to 2 tablespoons powdered sugar (sift after measuring)

1 large egg, beaten

BERRY TOPPING

About 2½ cups berries (a combination of raspberries and blueberries looks especially nice and is easy to slice)

¼ cup berry jam or preserves

Powdered sugar

There are several things to love about this tart, besides it being so darn easy. It looks "fancy" without needing a lot of know-how to make it; it easily breaks down into steps, which is a stress reliever; and no step during actual assembly needs to look perfect (that's the forgiveness part). This dessert shows off the berries. My version is not very sweet, but I've noted a couple of places you can up the sugar if desired. I keep a container of sugar with "used" vanilla beans buried in it to have on-demand vanilla sugar for my desserts.

You'll have some extra dough–I make cookies with it: Divide the dough into 10 to 12 pieces, roll into balls, place on a parchment-lined baking sheet, and press lightly to flatten to about ¼ inch thick. You can dredge first in white sugar and place back on the sheet. Bake at 350°F until lightly browned (check partway through baking time and rotate pan), for 10 to 13 minutes. Let cool for 5 to 10 minutes, then carefully remove from the pan. These cookies are fragile and buttery, with a hint of lemon. This leftover dough is handy to keep in your freezer, flattened and ready to be dredged and baked for last-minute cookie cravings. —MF

To make the Tart Dough, preheat the oven to 375°F. In the bowl of a food processor, mix the flour, sugar, salt, and lemon zest. Add the butter and process until a dough forms.

Take about half the dough and use your fingers to press it into the sides of a 9-inch tart pan with a removable bottom. The dough will shrink a little, so make sure it extends above the top of the ring a good ⅛ inch. Take about half of the remaining dough and press it firmly into the bottom of the pan. The walls should be slightly thicker than the base. The angle where the base of the wall meets the pan tends to get thicker during this process. Take a moment to press that area slightly to thin it a bit. Don't worry about making this look beautiful—the filling will cover any imperfections.

Bake the crust until richly golden brown, 18 to 22 minutes. Check during baking and turn the pan if the crust is browning unevenly. Remove from the oven and place on a wire rack to cool completely.

To make the Mascarpone Filling, preheat the oven to 375°F. Place the mascarpone, vanilla, and powdered sugar in a bowl. Using a rubber spatula, stir to blend, then thoroughly mix in the egg. Pour the mixture into the completely cooled tart shell and spread it evenly, picking up the pan and tilting it to help the thick filling cover the bottom. Bake the filling in the shell; the outside of the filling will puff up very slightly, but the inside may still appear soft, 12 to 15 minutes. Remove from the oven and cool completely on a wire rack.

When ready to assemble, rinse and gently dry the berries. Gently warm the jam for about 20 seconds in a microwave and pass it through a fine-mesh sieve to remove the seeds.

Cover the surface of the filling completely with tight concentric circles of berries. With a small pastry brush, paint the berries with the warmed jam. (If the jam seems too thick, stir in just a drop or two of water.) Be as painstaking as you'd like with this, but in the interest of ease, you don't need to go crazy.

Just before serving, use a fine-mesh sieve to sift powdered sugar lightly over the top of the tart. Serve within 3 hours to prevent the crust from softening.

Blackberry Crisp

MODERN BEAUJOLAIS

The blackberry crisp is a staple on the Cafe Beaujolais menu during the late summer months. At that time of year, the kitchen is inundated with wild blackberries from local foragers who bring bags full of the sun-ripened berries to our back door. This dessert is the epitome of what we stand for at Cafe Beaujolais: take the best seasonal ingredients, treat them simply, and let their true essence shine through. The topping is designed to provide enough for four crisps. It stays fresh in the refrigerator for up to 4 weeks and up to 3 months in the freezer, so you can easily put together a fruit crisp whenever you have fresh fruit on hand.

MAKES 4 TO 6 SERVINGS

CRISP TOPPING

½ cup hazelnuts

½ cup walnuts

½ cup pecans

2½ cups breadcrumbs

1 cup unsweetened shredded coconut

1½ cups firmly packed light brown sugar

1½ cups all-purpose flour

1¼ cups cold unsalted butter, cut into small chunks

2 pounds blackberries, wild preferred (about 7 cups)

½ cup granulated sugar

Vanilla Ice Cream (page 281), for serving

Preheat the oven to 350°F.

To make the topping, place all of the nuts onto a baking sheet and mix to distribute in a single layer. Bake until the nuts begin to brown and smell fragrant, about 10 minutes, stirring the nuts at the 5-minute mark. Remove from the oven and cool. Increase the oven temperature to 400°F.

Once the nuts are cooled, place the nuts in a food processor and pulse until roughly chopped. (This can also be done by hand with a knife on a cutting board.)

In a large bowl, combine the breadcrumbs, coconut, light brown sugar, and flour. Mix with a whisk until combined. Add the chopped nuts and butter chunks. Using your hands, mix the butter into the flour and nut mixture, squeezing to break up the pieces into smaller chunks. When ready, the mixture should resemble chunky sand with small pieces of butter along with semi larger chunks; there's no need to have a uniform mixture as the larger chunks of butter and smaller chunks will create texture in the final product.

In a medium bowl toss the blackberries with the sugar until well mixed. Pour the berry mixture into a 10-inch cast-iron skillet or 8 by 12-inch baking pan. Place 2 to 2½ cups of the topping over the berries, spreading it out evenly. Bake until the berry mixture is bubbling and the crisp topping is deeply browned, 30 to 40 minutes. Remove from the oven and let stand for 20 minutes.

Serve warm with scoops of ice cream.

MODERN BEAUJOLAIS

Vanilla Bean Panna Cotta with Summer Berries

MAKES 16 SERVINGS

- 3 cups heavy cream
- ½ cup milk
- ½ cup buttermilk
- ⅓ cup plus 2 tablespoons sugar
- ½ teaspoon fine sea salt
- 1 vanilla bean, split lengthwise and seeds scraped out
- 1 tablespoon gelatin
- 1 pound fresh raspberries
- 1 tablespoon water
- 2 teaspoons fresh lemon juice
- Assorted berries, for serving
- Fresh mint leaves, for garnish

I learned this recipe while working in Italy, where I learned that Italian cuisine thrives on simplicity. This classic dessert is the perfect example. Here in Mendocino, it is the perfect showcase for our summer berries. Chop up an assortment of strawberries, raspberries, blueberries, and blackberries for an incredible garnish to this summer classic. This is the perfect recipe to make for a crowd. Don't worry if you don't have 16 ramekins at the ready—the disposable aluminum ones work just fine.

In a saucepan over medium-low heat, warm the cream, milk, buttermilk, ⅓ cup sugar, salt, and vanilla bean pod and seeds until the mixture just comes to a simmer. Remove the saucepan from the heat, add the gelatin, and allow it to steep with the vanilla pod for 30 minutes, stirring occasionally.

Strain the mixture through a fine-mesh strainer into a bowl with a spout. Divide the mixture among sixteen 4-ounce ramekins. Chill in the refrigerator for at least 3 hours but preferably overnight.

In a saucepan, combine the raspberries, water, and remaining 2 tablespoons sugar. Set over medium-low heat and cook until the raspberries begin to break down, 4 to 5 minutes. You can smash the raspberries with a fork to speed up the process. Remove the mixture from the heat and add the lemon juice. Transfer the raspberry mixture to a high speed blender and blend on high until smooth. Strain through a fine-mesh strainer and chill in the refrigerator until serving time.

Using a small offset spatula or a butter knife, gently slide the spatula or knife down the side of each panna cotta. Slowly make a 360-degree turn to loosen the custard from the ramekin. Turn the ramekin upside down onto the serving plate or bowl. The panna cotta should release from its mold; if it doesn't initially, give it a couple taps while it's turned upside down. Serve each with raspberry sauce, fresh berries, and a fresh mint leaf.

Congo Bars, Revised

CLASSIC BEAUJOLAIS

What a surprise it was to discover that I wasn't still crazy about this recipe when I tested it for this recipe collection. It just seemed... blah. Since I'd baked more than 500 pans of these in my early days in Mendocino, I figured I had the recipe down. But no, so I made a few changes and voilà! A much better version, richer and loaded with more chips and walnuts. —MF

MAKES 24 BARS

- 1 cup plus 1 tablespoon unsalted butter, melted and cooled
- 2⅓ cups firmly packed light brown sugar
- 3 large farm-fresh eggs, beaten
- 2¾ cups all-purpose flour (stir to aerate before spooning into measuring cup)
- 2½ teaspoons baking powder
- ¾ teaspoon fine sea salt
- 2 cups (12 ounce package) semisweet (46%) chocolate chips (I use Guittard)
- 2 cups walnuts, toasted, cooled, and coarsely chopped

Preheat the oven to 325°F. Using 1 tablespoon of the melted butter, grease a 10 by 15-inch baking pan well.

In a large bowl, use a wooden spoon to blend together the remaining 1 cup butter, sugar, and eggs. In a separate bowl, mix together the flour, baking powder, and salt. Add the flour mixture to the butter mixture, stir to blend, then stir in the chocolate chips and walnuts until thoroughly mixed. Transfer the batter to the prepared pan. (This batter is very sticky, so you may need to pat it out evenly with your fingers.) Bake for 25 minutes, then turn the pan to ensure even baking.

The next 5 to 10 minutes are the most crucial because you must avoid overbaking these bars to ensure a heavenly texture. The dough will have puffed up at the 25-minute mark, then it settles down. It will be under done in the center at this point, but in about 5 minutes, pull it out and cool on a rack. You may have to make this a second time to fine-tune your assessment, but hey, that's not a bad thing, right?

When cool, cut into 24 bars.

MODERN BEAUJOLAIS

Saltine Crunch

MAKES 12 TO 14 SERVINGS

- 1½ cups sliced almonds
- About 60 saltine crackers
- 1½ cups sugar
- 1½ cups unsalted butter
- 2 tablespoons corn syrup
- 1 cinnamon stick
- 3 bay leaves
- Juice of ½ lemon
- ½ pound dark chocolate (60%), chopped into small chunks

I grew up in a household in which home cooking was prized. This recipe, a riff on toffee, was one of my mother's specialties. It is a salty-sweet treat that always brings a smile to my face. As a kid, I had a wicked sweet tooth. When my mom made this, I would stay up late and sneak down to the kitchen and devour a few of these yummy treats and then quietly retreat back to my bedroom. Since my youth, I've discovered that this recipe is perfect to make and bring to a potluck dinner if you need to throw together something in a pinch.

Preheat the oven to 350°F. Line a baking sheet with a silicone baking mat.

Pour the sliced almonds evenly on an unlined baking sheet and bake in the oven until lightly golden, 5 to 7 minutes.

Arrange the saltine crackers on the prepared baking sheet in a single layer, making sure there are no holes or large gaps. You can break crackers in half to patch up any areas as needed.

In a saucepan combine the sugar, butter, corn syrup, cinnamon, bay leaves, and lemon juice. Cook over medium-low heat until the sugar begins to melt. Continue to cook over medium-low heat without stirring for about 5 minutes or until the mixture begins to brown on the edges of the saucepan. Reduce the heat to low and insert a candy thermometer into the mixture. Let the mixture continue to cook until it registers 300°F, about 5 more minutes.

Carefully remove the cinnamon stick and bay leaves. Wearing oven mitts to protect your hands and arms, slowly pour the caramel mixture over the crackers. Evenly sprinkle the chopped chocolate over the caramel and cracker mixture, which will melt from the heat of the caramel. Scatter the toasted almonds over the chocolate and place the baking sheet into the refrigerator to cool and set, about 30 minutes.

Remove the baking sheet from the refrigerator. Using a long, sharp knife, cut the toffee into irregular triangular pieces, about 15 to 20 one-inch pieces.

Vanilla Ice Cream with Variations

This ice cream recipe is the best one I have come across. It always is soft and silky and never has icy crystals or off-putting textures. Once you understand how to impart flavors into the basic mixture, the sky's the limit for possible flavors. Invert sugar, a type of sugar with a special chemical structure, as opposed to regular sugar, gives uniform sweetness and mitigates the problem of sugar crystals in your finished ice cream. You can source invert sugar easily on food specialty websites.

MAKES 2 QUARTS

4 cups half-and-half

1 vanilla bean, split lengthwise and seeds scraped

16 large egg yolks

1¾ cup granulated sugar

7 ounces invert sugar

4 cups heavy cream

1½ teaspoon vanilla extract

In a saucepan, combine the half-and-half and vanilla bean and seeds. Place over medium heat until the mixture just comes to a simmer. Remove from the heat, cover, and let the vanilla infuse into the half-and-half for 15 minutes.

Fill a large bowl with ice. Transfer the half-and-half mixture to a large bowl, removing the vanilla bean with kitchen tongs, and set it in the ice to cool down. Stir the mixture frequently to help it cool down quickly and at an even rate.

While the mixture cools, put the egg yolks, granulated sugar, and invert sugar in a stand mixer fitted with the whisk attachment. Mix on high speed until the mixture turns a very pale yellow and doubles in size, 7 to 10 minutes. Transfer the egg yolk mixture to a clean saucepan along with the heavy cream and vanilla and set the saucepan on the stovetop over medium heat. Cook, stirring the mixture constantly, until an instant-read thermometer inserted into the mixture registers 178°F. Pour the heated mixture through a chinois or strainer directly into the bowl with the half-and-half. Cool the mixture in the ice bath, stirring from time to time, until it reaches 45°F. Then, cover the bowl and transfer the mixture to the refrigerator to chill overnight.

When you're ready to churn, follow the manufacturer's instructions for your ice cream maker. Once the ice cream thickens, transfer it to storage containers and freeze it until ready to serve.

Ice Cream Variations

Triple Ginger Ice Cream

This is an amazing wintertime ice cream recipe. I use three different types of ginger for this recipe: dried, candied, and fresh.

Follow the recipe for Vanilla Ice Cream on page 281, substituting ½ cup peeled and freshly grated ginger for the vanilla bean and 1 tablespoon ground ginger in place of the vanilla extract. When churning the ice cream in the ice cream maker, 1 minute before you remove the ice cream from the machine, sprinkle in ½ cup candied ginger pieces.

Frozen Lemon Custard

This recipe is a delicious addition to your ice cream repertoire. Here, I infuse lemon curd into the ice cream base for a refreshing twist on ice cream.

Follow the recipe for Vanilla Ice Cream on page 281, omitting the vanilla bean and the vanilla extract. Once the mixture has been chilled in the ice bath in the final step before churning and chilling overnight, blend 2 cups Lemon Curd (see page 293) into the ice cream base with an immersion blender.

Mint Chip Ice Cream

One of my favorite variations on vanilla ice cream is mint chip, featuring garden-fresh mint. I use extremely high-quality bittersweet chocolate chunks to balance out the herbal notes of the mint.

Follow the recipe for Vanilla Ice Cream on page 281 but omit the vanilla bean. Instead, add 1 cup loosely packed fresh mint leaves and increase the steeping time from 15 minutes to 30 minutes and strain the mint leaves with a fine-mesh strainer before chilling.

After churning the ice cream in the last step, fold in 1 cup bittersweet (75%) chocolate chunks or wafers to the finished ice cream before packing it into storage containers.

Chocolate Chip Cookies

These cookies have been on our Waiting Room menu and for sale at our pizza window since we opened the new incarnation of Cafe Beaujolais. Many home cooks are familiar with the classic Toll House recipe, but I developed this version to be crisper on the outside, yet still chewy and soft on the inside. The best part is that the dough can be made ahead of time, portioned into balls, and frozen. They will last for up to 3 months and can be baked off on demand.

MAKES 2 DOZEN LARGE COOKIES

- 1 pound unsalted butter, melted and cooled
- 1⅓ cups granulated sugar
- 1⅓ cups firmly packed dark brown sugar
- 1 tablespoon vanilla extract
- 1 tablespoon fine sea salt
- 4 extra-large farm-fresh eggs, at room temperature
- 2¼ cups pastry flour
- 2¼ cups all-purpose flour
- 1 tablespoon baking soda
- 3 cups dark chocolate (65% or more) chunks
- 1 cup walnuts, toasted (see page 295)

Preheat the oven to 350°F. Line 3 baking sheets with parchment paper.

Put the cooled melted butter into a mixing bowl. Add the granulated sugar, brown sugar, vanilla, and salt and mix with a rubber spatula until a paste is formed. Add the eggs and gently mix together.

In another bowl, sift together the 2 flours and baking soda. In two equal batches, add the flour and the butter mixture to the bowl of a stand mixer fitted with the paddle attachment. Mix on medium-low speed until the dough is firm but not wet, about 3 minutes, taking care not to overmix. Fold in the chocolate chunks and walnuts.

Using a cookie scoop, scoop the cookie batter onto the prepared baking sheets, leaving about 3 inches between each dough ball. Bake until the edges of the cookies just begin to brown and crisp up, about 20 minutes. Be sure to not overbake these cookies! Remove from the oven and let the cookies cool on the baking sheets for 5 minutes. Then, use a spatula to transfer the cookies to a wire rack to cool completely.

DE CAFÉ

Thanksgiving Coffee

SUPPLIER SPOTLIGHT

For more than 50 years, Paul and Joan Katzeff have believed that the secret to great coffee lies in the welfare of the farmers who grow it. Sourcing directly from small-scale farmer cooperatives from coffee growing regions throughout the world, they developed co-beneficial relationships with farmers spanning decades. Their unique ethical sourcing model (which was used as the basis for the first Fairtrade certification) has given them and us access to rare and acclaimed coffees that you can't find elsewhere.

Thanksgiving Coffee was already an institution when Chef Margaret Fox took ownership of Cafe Beaujolais in 1977. The restaurant became home to the very first espresso machine on the Mendocino Coast, and the two businesses collaborated on a custom Cafe Beaujolais blend. The partnership enhanced Thanksgiving Coffee's brand and retail business as the special blend was an immediate hit and remains a retail bestseller to this day.

Forty-three years later, while laying the groundwork for The Waiting Room, we realized the need for a new and improved Beaujolais Blend and we were excited to also strengthen the relationship between Thanksgiving and Beaujolais. We visited Thanksgiving's coffee lab, discussed our wishes, and collaborated to design our own custom roasts. In fact, every three months, I go to Thanksgiving's roastery to develop a new seasonal coffee with Jacob, their master roaster. We select the coffee bean origin, dial in roast levels, and taste and tweak until we get things just right. It's an amazing opportunity that allows me to approach our coffee selections just like our seasonal food menus. In the winter, for example, we may pull more chocolate flavors out of Nicaraguan beans, and in the summer, we may opt for bright Ethiopian beans that boast flavors of blueberry and plum. We're humbled to influence Thanksgiving's diversified roast style, especially as the business enters its newest chapter with Paul and Joan's son, Jonah, at the helm.

The award-winning, Certified B Corp, second-generation family-owned business truly stands behind its motto, "Not Just a Cup, But a Just Cup." Thanksgiving Coffee's accomplishments are as abundant as the Katzeff's hearts, and we'd be remiss to not mention at least a few:

- Thanksgiving introduced the first Certified Organic coffee line in 1990, followed by some of the first single-origin coffees in 1992;
- Paul worked with USAID to introduce the first farmer-owned cupping labs in small cooperatives in Nicaragua. This gave farmers the new opportunity to taste and improve their own coffees, thus understanding the true value of their product, and enabling them to attain fair market prices for their beans;
- The name Thanksgiving Coffee reflects the Katzeff's gratitude for living in a place where nature's cornucopia overflows. The ideals of the holiday resonated with their founders: community, abundance, giving back, and giving thanks for our bounty.

Cafe Beajolais's coffee comes from the kindest industry legends!

While we'd love to see you at The Waiting Room, where we offer retail bags of our custom seasonal blends, we also encourage you to visit Thanksgiving Coffee's online store, where a single purchase can support one of many great environmental causes.

Chocolate Budinos with Mascarpone Cream

MAKES 8 SERVINGS

CHOCOLATE BUDINOS

1 cup heavy cream

1 cup whole milk

6 large egg yolks

¼ cup granulated sugar

¾ teaspoon fine sea salt

1 cup bittersweet (65%) chocolate disks (Tcho brand is great)

MASCARPONE CREAM

½ cup mascarpone

½ cup powdered sugar

1 tablespoon vanilla extract, or 1 vanilla bean, split lengthwise and seeds scraped

1 cup heavy cream

Chocolate shavings, for serving

Fresh berries, for serving

4 tablespoons extra-virgin olive oil, for drizzling

This is a rotating dessert on the Cafe Beaujolais menu. Unassuming, these bring back memories of the pudding cups I enjoyed during middle school, though these are decidedly adult versions of the treats. The olive oil brings an extra-special intrigue and balances the sweetness of the dessert.

To make the Chocolate Budinos, in a saucepan over medium heat, warm the cream and milk until the mixture just comes to a simmer. Remove from the heat.

In a stand mixer fitted with the whisk attachment, or by hand with a whisk, whip the egg yolks, sugar, and salt until the mixture becomes a pale yellow color, 2 to 3 minutes. While whisking, slowly ladle the hot milk mixture into the egg yolk mixture, starting with a drizzle and then progressively adding the milk at a quicker rate. Once the milk has been fully combined with the egg yolk mixture, pour it back into the pan and place it over medium-low heat. Cook, stirring constantly and scraping the sides of the pan with a heatproof rubber spatula, until an instant-read thermometer reaches 175°F, about 5 minutes. Remove the mixture from the heat and pour into a clean bowl along with the bittersweet chocolate. Let stand for 5 minutes.

Using an immersion blender or whisk, blend the chocolate with the egg-milk mixture. Divide the mixture among 8 small glasses, cups, or bowls and chill in the refrigerator for a minimum of 2 hours or up to 3 days.

To make the Mascarpone Cream, in a stand mixer fitted with the whisk attachment, beat the mascarpone on medium speed until completely smooth. Add the powdered sugar and vanilla extract. Continue to beat, slowly drizzling the cream into the mascarpone mixture. Do not add the cream too quickly, or the mascarpone will separate, creating a lumpy texture. Whisk until the cream is almost stiff peaks.

To serve, remove the budinos from the refrigerator and top with a generous scoop of mascarpone cream. Top with the chocolate shavings, fresh berries, and a couple teaspoons each of olive oil.

Stocks, Sauces & Staples

Beaujolais Blend Herbs

When I was the proprietor of Cafe Beaujolais, we had a signature spice blend that we used in many of our dishes. It is no longer available for sale, but this blend approximates the flavor. —MF

MAKES ABOUT 2 TABLESPOONS

2 generous pinches dried basil

2 generous pinches dried oregano

2 generous pinches dried thyme

1 generous pinch dried tarragon

1 generous pinch dried rosemary

Mix the herbs together and put in an airtight jar.

Cajun Bleu Seasoning

This is an interesting seasoning that I found while working at a restaurant in Spokane, Washington, while attending university. I love the addition of bleu cheese powder, which adds umami to the mix. Don't worry if you are not a bleu cheese fan, as it is just there for seasoning and not as prominent a flavor as you might think.

MAKES 1 CUP

3 tablespoons paprika

3 tablespoons dried bleu cheese (Hidden Valley bleu cheese packets work)

2 tablespoons fine sea salt

2 tablespoons garlic powder

1 tablespoon black pepper

1 tablespoon ground white pepper

1 tablespoon onion powder

1 tablespoon dried oregano

1 tablespoon cayenne pepper

½ tablespoon dried thyme

Mix all the ingredients together and store in an airtight container until ready for use.

Frying Eggs

Preheat a nonstick pan over medium-low heat and add ½ teaspoon of coconut oil or grapeseed oil. Crack the eggs into the pan and cook undisturbed until the white has cooked and the yolk is runny, 2 to 3 minutes for sunny-side-up eggs, or until cooked to your liking.

Lemon Confit

Otherwise known as preserved lemons, these flavor bombs add amazing pops of tanginess and umami to a variety of dishes.

MAKES 12 TO 16 PRESERVED LEMONS

2 cups fine sea salt

½ cup granulated sugar

12 to 16 whole Meyer lemons, rinsed and dried

In a bowl, mix together the sugar and salt. Using a sharp knife, quarter the lemons from the top down, stopping about ½ inch from the bottom to keep the base intact to create 4 wedges that are being held together at the bottom of the fruit.

Put the cut lemons in the bowl with the salt-sugar mixture. Using your hands liberally massage the salt-sugar mixture into the interior of the fruit. Place the coated lemons into a large mason jar or another similarly sized container with a lid. Sprinkle a bit of the salt and sugar mixture atop the lemons. Repeat these steps until all of the lemons have been added to the container. Place the remainder of the salt and sugar mixture on top to create almost a "salt lid," being sure that the lemons are completely covered by the salt-sugar mixture. Place the lid onto the container and allow it to sit out at room temperature for a minimum of 2 weeks and up to 1 year. For best results, use after 3 months.

Lemon Curd

I use this tangy citrus curd in both my Lemon Cheesecake (page 262) and my Frozen Lemon Custard (page 282). It's also delicious on scones and other baked goods.

MAKES 1 CUP

1½ cups sugar

Finely grated zest of 3 lemons

½ cup unsalted butter, at room temperature

4 large farm-fresh eggs

½ cup fresh lemon juice

Put the sugar and lemon zest in a food processor and blend until a fine, sand-like texture forms. Add the butter and eggs and blend until combined. Transfer the mixture to a saucepan and add the lemon juice. Place over medium-low heat and warm, whisking constantly, until the mixture begins to thicken, about 10 minutes.

Strain the mixture through a fine-mesh sieve into a clean bowl. Place a piece of plastic wrap directly on the surface of the curd (this will prevent it from developing a "skin" on the surface) and refrigerate until ready to use. It will last for about 5 days in the refrigerator.

Melting Chocolate

Fill a saucepan with about 1½ inches of water and place over medium heat until it barely simmers. Place a heatproof bowl on top, making sure it doesn't touch the water below. Put the chopped chocolate in the bowl. Heat the chocolate, stirring often with a silicone spatula, until melted and smooth, 3 to 4 minutes. Protecting your hands, lift out the bowl and use the melted chocolate as needed. Note: chocolate can seize when it comes into contact with moisture. Take care to keep water or steam away from the chocolate.

Pickled Fresno Chiles

Use these pickled chiles to accompany anything you want to add a tangy-spicy-sweet flavor. I recommend sourcing the peppers during peak ripeness in the late summer months.

1 pound Fresno chiles, stems removed

1 cup rice vinegar

1 cup water

½ cup sugar

1 tablespoon fine sea salt

Slice the chiles thinly into rounds and place into a mason jar or heatproof container with a lid. Place the vinegar, water, sugar, and salt into a medium saucepan. Turn the burner on high heat and bring the mixture to a boil. Once boiling, remove the pan from the heat and pour the mixture over the chopped chiles. Let the chiles cool on the counter until room temperature. Then, seal the container and refrigerate. The pickled chiles are ready for use after 2 days and will last for up to 3 months in the refrigerator.

Raita

Raitas are yogurt-based accompaniments served in India as cooling companions to spicy dishes. I serve this with my Universal-Style Indian Curry (page 172).

MAKES ABOUT 2 CUPS

¾ cup grated peeled and seeded cucumber

1 cup plain Greek yogurt

Juice of 1 lemon

¼ cup chopped fresh cilantro

2 teaspoons fine sea salt, or to taste

Place the grated cucumber in a clean kitchen towel. Bring the ends of the towel together and squeeze the cucumber through the towel to remove as much liquid as possible. Place the drained cucumber in a bowl. Add the yogurt, lemon juice, chopped cilantro, and salt. Stir to blend. Taste and adjust the seasoning.

Margaret's Sweet Spice Mixture

I love this combination of spices so much that I add it into oatmeal, coffee drinks, hot chocolate, and blend with butter to spread on toast. In the interest of ease, except for the nutmeg (there's such a difference when freshly grated), all the spices are ground. If you prefer and have the time, purchase whole spices, and grind them. In any case, make sure all your spices are fresh and fragrant. —MF

MAKES ABOUT 2½ TABLESPOONS

1 tablespoon ground ginger

2 teaspoons cinnamon

1 teaspoon freshly grated nutmeg

1 teaspoon ground cardamom

1½ teaspoons ground cloves

Blend the spices together, then transfer to a small glass jar and store away from the light.

Beef Stock

Beef bones can be purchased from your local butcher shop and should be cut up into manageable pieces so that they can fit in your home oven and stock pot. Beef knuckle bones are the best option for this recipe, as they provide the most flavor.

MAKES 6 TO 7 QUARTS

5 pounds beef bones

4 tablespoons tomato paste

4 carrots, peeled

2 onions, peeled and halved

1 bunch celery

4 bay leaves, fresh preferred

2 tablespoons whole black peppercorns

1 bunch parsley stems

1 bunch fresh thyme

8 quarts ice water

Preheat the oven to 350°F.

Place the beef bones onto a rimmed baking sheet and roast until evenly browned, about 30 minutes. Remove the bones from the oven and transfer to a 12-quart stock pot. Drain the excess fat from the baking sheet and discard. Using a metal spatula, scrape the browned bits from the bottom of the pan and add them to the stock pot. Place a small sauté pan on medium-low heat and add the tomato paste. Cook the tomato paste for 3 to 5 minutes, stirring occasionally. Once the tomato paste begins to slightly brown, add the paste to the bones in the stock pot. Add the carrots, onions, celery, bay leaves, black peppercorns, parsley stems, thyme, and ice water to the stock pot. Place over high heat and bring to a boil. Once the stock is boiling, reduce the heat to low and simmer for 3 hours.

Carefully remove the beef bones from the stock pot and discard. Strain the stock through a fine-mesh sieve into a large bowl and allow it to cool completely on the countertop. The stock can be used immediately or placed in an airtight container and refrigerated for up to 10 days or frozen for up to 3 months.

Chicken Stock

Homemade stocks are one of the secret weapons of any chef. Making your own stock at home is far superior to anything store-bought. I never add salt to my stocks as this allows me to have much more freedom to accurately adjust the salt level in whichever recipe calls for stock. This is the most simple chicken stock recipe, but it delivers the flavor needed to enhance any recipe.

MAKES 4 TO 5 QUARTS

4 pounds chicken bones

4 carrots, peeled

2 onions, peeled and halved

1 bunch celery

4 bay leaves, fresh preferred

2 tablespoons whole black peppercorns

1 bunch fresh parsley stems

6 quarts ice water

Preheat the oven to 350°F.

Place the chicken bones on a rimmed baking sheet and roast until evenly browned, about 30 minutes.

Remove the bones from the oven and transfer to an 8-quart stock pot. Drain the excess fat from the baking sheet and discard. Using a metal spatula, scrape the browned bits from the bottom of the pan and add them to the stock pot. Place the carrots, onions, celery, bay leaves, black peppercorns, parsley stems, and ice water into the stock pot. Place over high heat and bring to a boil. Once the stock is boiling, reduce the heat to low and simmer for 90 minutes.

Carefully remove the chicken bones from the stock pot and discard. Strain the stock through a fine-mesh sieve into a large bowl and allow it to cool completely on the countertop. The stock can be used immediately or placed in an airtight container and refrigerated for up to 10 days or frozen for up to 3 months.

Fish Stock

You want to plan ahead when making fish stock, as an overnight soak helps purge the bones of any impurities.

MAKES 4 TO 5 QUARTS

4 pounds white or neutral-tasting fish bones, such as rock fish, halibut, black cod, or sole, cleaned of blood and skin

6 quarts ice water

4 carrots, peeled and cut into ½-inch pieces

2 onions, peeled and quartered

2 shallots, split lengthwise

2 bay leaves, fresh preferred

1 tablespoon whole black peppercorns

1 bunch fresh parsley stems

The night before you want to make the stock, place the fish bones into an 8-quart stock pot and fill with water. Place the pot into the refrigerator and allow the bones to sit for a minimum of 8 hours. This allows the impurities to be pulled out of the bones, creating a clearer, more balanced stock.

The next day, when you are ready to make the stock, remove the fish bones from the water. Discard the soaking water and refill the stock pot with the fresh ice water. Add the carrots, onions, shallots, bay leaves, peppercorns, and parsley stems to the pot. Set the pot over high heat and bring the liquid to a boil. Once the stock is boiling, reduce the heat to low and simmer for 1 hour

Carefully remove the fish bones from the stock pot and discard. Strain the stock through a fine-mesh sieve and allow it to cool completely on the countertop. The stock can be used immediately or placed in an airtight container and refrigerated for up to 10 days or frozen for up to 3 months.

Toasting Nuts or Seeds

Place the nuts or seeds in a dry frying pan over medium heat. Let them cook, stirring occasionally and watching them closely, until the nuts or seeds are golden brown, 2 to 3 minutes. When golden, transfer the nuts or seeds to a plate to stop the cooking.

Toasting Coconut

Preheat the oven to 350°F. Spread the coconut into a single layer on a rimmed baking sheet. Bake until light golden brown, stirring occasionally, 8 to 10 minutes. Remove from the oven and transfer to a plate to stop the cooking.

INDEX

D

E

F

G

H

I

J

K

L

M

N

O

P

Q

R

S

T

V

W

Y

Z

CONVERSION CHART

All recipes in this cookbook use standard U.S. measurements. There are many measurement conversion websites that give precise equivalents, which may be especially helpful for baked goods. The conversions below have been rounded up or down for convenience. For most recipes the slight difference will be undetectable.

U.S. VOLUME TO METRIC

General rule—each fluid (liquid) ounce equals about 30 milliliters

U.S. VOLUME	METRIC
⅛ teaspoon	0.5 ml (milliliter)
¼ teaspoon	1 ml
½ teaspoon	2 ml
¾ teaspoon	4 ml
1 teaspoon	5 ml
1 tablespoon (3 tsp)	15 ml
¼ cup (2 oz., 4 tbsp)	60 ml
⅓ cup (3 oz.)	75 ml
½ cup (4 oz.)	120 ml
¾ cup (6 oz.)	180 ml
1 cup (8 oz.)	240 ml
2 cups (16 oz., 1 U.S. pint)	480 ml
1 quart (32 oz., 4 cups)	1 L (liter)

U.S. WEIGHT TO METRIC

General rule—each ounce equals about 28 grams

U.S. WEIGHT	METRIC
½ ounce	15 g (grams)
1 ounce	30 g
¼ pound (4 ounces)	115 g
½ pound (8 ounces)	225 g
1 pound (16 ounces)	450 g
2¼ pounds	1 kg (kilogram)

U.S. LENGTH TO METRIC

U.S. LENGTH	METRIC
⅛ inch	3 mm (millimeters)
¼ inch	5 mm
½ inch	1.25 cm (centimeters)
¾ inch	2 cm
1 inch	2.5 cm
12 inches (1 foot)	30 cm

FAHRENHEIT TO CELSIUS OR GAS MARK

F	250°	300°	350°	375°	400°	425°	450°	475°	500°
C	120°	150°	180°	190°	200°	220°	230°	240°	260°
GAS MARK	½	2	4	5	6	7	8	9	10

If using a fan-assist (convection) oven, reduce temperatures by 25°F or 20°C or as directed by the manufacturer instructions. Timing may vary.

ACKNOWLEDGMENTS

The life of a chef and a business owner can be summed up as a literal journey of ups and downs, highs and lows, hills and valleys. It has been a wild ride that has ultimately culminated into my writing this cookbook. This will go down as one of the many chapters in my culinary career, one that would not have been possible without the support of the many in my circle and the support of the thousands of customers that have dined with us at the Beaujolais. I will not be able to include all of my thanks to the many people but I will try my best.

Thanks to my family: Peter, Melissa, Samantha, Jacob, Grandpo Joe, Grandma Christina and Grammy Carol, for their caring, financial and emotional support, constructive criticism, patience and love; Margaret Fox for taking me under her wing and unabashed support during the transition and expansion of her restaurant; David LaMonica, the most recent owner of the Cafe, for his willingness to always answer questions about almost anything and everything; Linda Friedman for her staunch support and genuine love of Cafe Beaujolais as well as coming up with "The Waiting Room" as the unique and apropos name for our coffee shop; Rachel Lopez Metzger for approaching me and coaching me through the writing and designing of this book; Jennifer Newens for her editing; Chef Charles Olalia for teaching me the intricacies of fine dining and leadership; Chef Jeremy Hansen for taking me under his wing during my college years and inspiring a love for food and quality; Chef Gino Angelini for his patience and openness to teaching me his skills; the locals of the Mendocino Coast for being the most amazing customers any chef and business owner could ask for; Chef Luis Lopez for being the rock that this restaurant has leaned on for over 30 years; the entire Beaujolais staff who have been with me every step of the way; the most talented servers Maritha Kerwin and Janet Atherton who have been a part of the Beaujolais story for longer than I have; Daniela Tallman for organizing and inspiring the amazing photographs in this book; Leah Hammerman for her assistance and direction in developing and writing the chapter introductions and the supplier spotlight sections; Mark Bowery who inspired my knowledge and love for wine and who also worked under Margaret Fox at the Cafe; our dishwashers: German, Alvaro, and Santos who have also been a part of the Beaujolais story longer than I have. This story is for all of you and I hope I do you proud with the writing of this cookbook so that we can share a part of the Beaujolais story to the world.

ABOUT THE AUTHOR

Julian Lopez is the head chef, wine buyer, and co-owner of Cafe Beaujolais in Mendocino, California. His culinary adventure has taken him to restaurants in southern France, northern and central Italy, Los Angeles, California, and Spokane, Washington where he has learned various cooking techniques that have defined his cooking style. His culinary philosophy is based on his desire to transport diners to their earliest memories of food, whether that be a home-cooked meal from family or an unpretentious meal from a neighborhood eatery. He firmly believes that food is intrinsically linked to memory, and the ability to tap into those memories is what creates amazing culinary experiences. His sincere wish is that this cookbook will allow each reader the ability to create food memories that they will hand down from generation to generation.

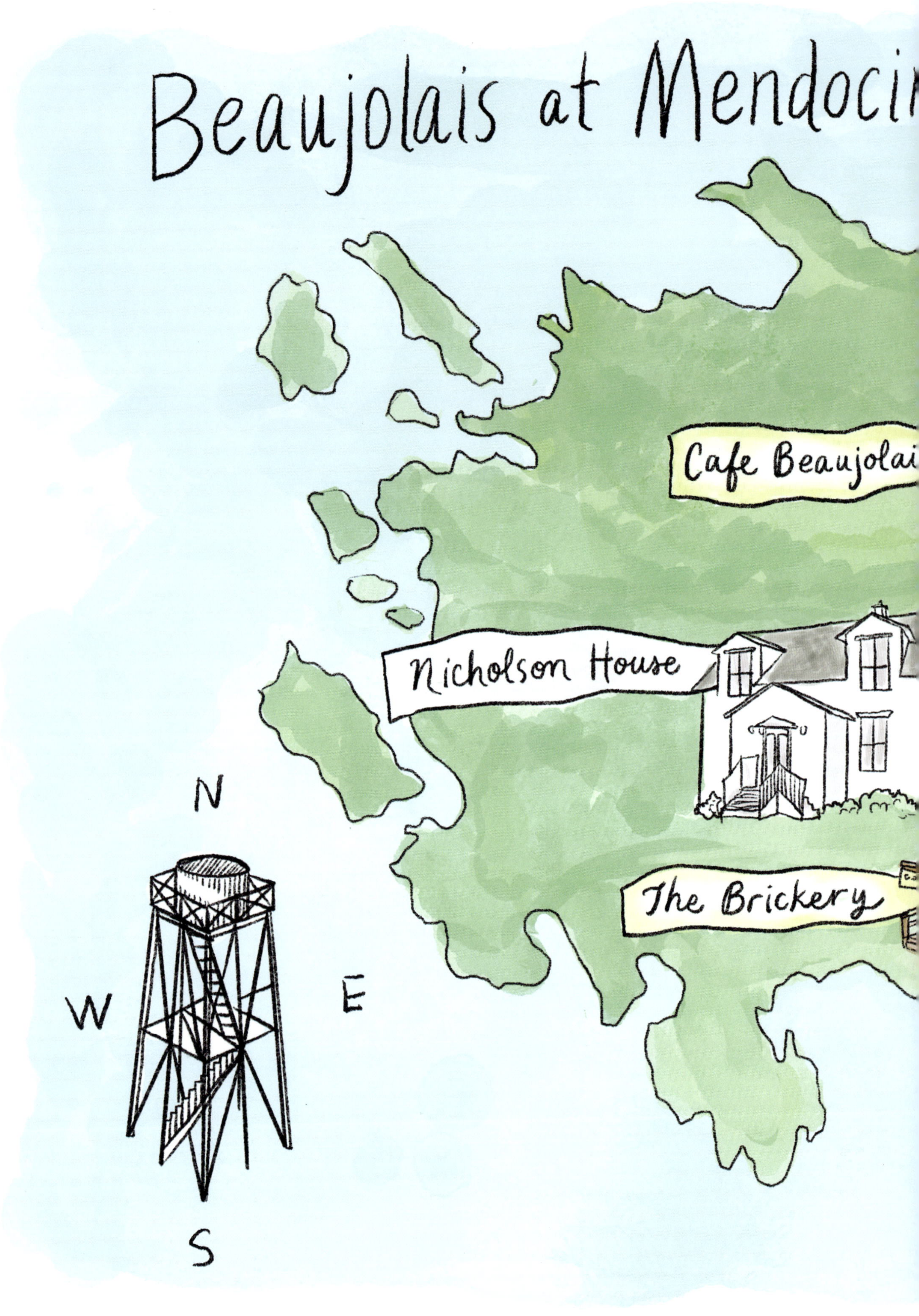

Beaujolais at Mendoci

Cafe Beaujolai

Nicholson House

The Brickery

N

W

E

S